Developing Church Leaders

Understanding and Nurturing Leadership in the Local Church

Dr. James A. Hinkle

Copyright © 2011 Dr. James A. Hinkle. All rights reserved. This material may not be reproduced without the author's written consent.

Unless otherwise noted, all scripture quotations are from The Holy Bible: New International Version. Copyright © 1973. Used by permission of Zondervan Bible Publishers.

James may be contacted via email: James@burnschurchofchrist.org

Biography

In his own words, James was born in "1900-and-none-of-your-business" in Limestone County, Alabama. Fast-forward to 2010 and you'll find James still active in his 50th year of ministry.

He has been a constant servant of the Lord's church, dedicating many years of thoughtful study and preparation to help others lead. James earned his bachelor's degree from Lipscomb University in Nashville, his master's degree from Harding University Graduate School of Religion in Memphis, and his D.Min. from Fuller Seminary in Pasadena, California.

In his years of service, he's helped churches in Tennessee, Wisconsin, Nebraska, Hawaii, New Zealand, the United Kingdom, and in Africa. Additionally, he has served on faculty at York College in York, Nebraska, as a visiting professor at the South Pacific Bible College in Tauranga, New Zealand, and as a counselor and family minister for the Walnut Street Church of Christ in Dickson, Tennessee. He co-authored *Among Friends: You can help make your church a warmer place* with Tim Woodroof, and has conducted seminars across the nation.

James's most recent service has been with the Burns Church of Christ in Burns, Tennessee. He began his work with Burns in a difficult time, but his leadership helped the church grow in the aftermath of some difficulties. He continues to serve the church there as an elder.

James is a rare breed in ministers. His longevity, diversity, academic training, and personal kindness have made him exceptionally effective. You will be blessed by your reading of this book.

James can be reached at james@burnschurchofchrist.org.

Table of Contents

Biography 3
Table of Contents 5
Author's Preface 9
Editors' Foreword 10
Chapter 1 The Purpose and Function of Ministry 11
    All Talk, No Action? 11
    "What is a minister?" 12
    Grace-Based Ministry 12
    Ministry Words 14
    Discussion Questions 17
Chapter 2 Building a Team 19
    From Putting out Fires to Casting Vision 19
    Ingredients for a Good Team 20
    Discussion Questions 28
Chapter 3 The What and Why of Team Building 29
    A Learned Skill: The "What" 29
    Learn from the Masters 30
    The "Why" of Team Building 32
    Discussion Questions 39
Chapter 4 Good Team, Bad Team 41
    Team Agenda vs. Personal Agenda 41
    Interdependent vs. Independent vs. Overdependent 42
    Consumer Church Quiz 45

Sense of Purpose vs. Just a Job 46

Self Starters vs. Sitters and Waiters 47

Innovative vs. Conservative 48

Helping Hands vs. "Not My Job" 48

Enjoy vs. Irritate 50

Thriving on Adventure vs. Running from Risks 51

Discussion Questions 52

Chapter 5 Finding the Real Disease 53

Making the Diagnosis 53

Looking Beyond the Symptoms 54

The Real Problem 61

Steps to Good Health 62

Discussion Questions 64

Chapter 6 Two Continuums: Tasks vs. Relationships and Goals vs. People 65

Goal-Oriented Leaders 65

People-Oriented Leaders 68

Discovering Your Leadership Style 70

Discussion Questions 76

Chapter 7 What Kind of Leader Will You Follow? 77

Compassion 77

Preparation 79

Faithfulness 81

Service 83

Problem Solvers 83

Empathetic 84

Non-Judgmental Listening 85

Prayer 86

Motivate 87

Enthusiasm 88

Discussion Questions 89

Chapter 8 Choosing a Model for Leadership 91

Finding Our Leadership Styles 92

The Leader's Charge 93

Ex Officio or De Facto? 95

What are our goals? 97

How much time and energy do we have? 99

How much do you care? 100

What are our priorities? 101

What is our philosophy of leadership? 102

What promotes maturity, commitment, and involvement? 103

Discussion Questions 104

Chapter 9 Committing Others to the Work 105

Welcome Ideas 106

Accept Mistakes 106

Hold Your Temper 107

Learn When to Let Go 108

Testing Your Ability to Delegate 111

Discussion Questions 113

Chapter 10 Leadership Styles 115

Finding a Style 115

    Leadership Style One: Laissez-faire (1, 1) 118

    Leadership Style Two: Autocratic (9, 1) 120

    Leadership Style Three: Authoritative (7, 3) 123

    Leadership Style Four: Democratic (5, 5) 125

    Leadership Style Five: Rapport (1, 9) 129

    Discussion Questions 130

Chapter 11 A New Old Style of Leadership 131

    A "Third Way" 131

    Characteristics of Maieutic Leaders 134

    Discussion Questions 141

Bibliography 143

Author's Preface

There is no end to books on church leadership. I will chance to add another to the long list. We may talk about leadership until we turn blue but we still haven't been real successful in leadership training.

Any book that can give you one good, workable idea is worth reading and spending some quality time in spiritual reflection. Reading and thinking about the precepts presented in this book can help you become a better leader and help your church be a better place.

The ideas presented in this book have been tried and tested. They have been presented in many seminars and workshops. I have received feedback and honed the principles so they are now ready to be exposed to a new reading clientele. Thank you for being one of the readers. My prayer is that many will find new ways of developing leaders in local churches.

I was surprised at a special dinner with the first proofs of this book. Keith Oliver and Matthew Hiatt did the work of taking the material that I had written and putting it together in publishable form. My wife Harriett and Matthew worked on this proof and improved it considerably. They did this by phone and email as Harriett and I travelled from Tennessee to California. They are working on the rewrites as I write this forward in Laughlin, NV. Isn't modern technology great?

I want to especially thank Matthew Hiatt for doing yeoman's work to get this book to the press. Matthew and I have worked together for several years and I have found him a worthy co-worker. If this book is used by the reader to make the church a better place, we have received our reward. God's church is the greatest institution in our world and we need to lead in God's way and in a dynamic fashion.

This book is not intended for easy reading. Much study of the principles shared in the pages of this book can lead to better leadership and better churches. This is especially true with the last two chapters. Grids are not common for those out of industry and education, but are helpful to those who spend the necessary time studying them. Spend the time necessary to capture the principles contained herein and you can become a better leader that equips the body for works of service. Churches can never rise above its leaders. Let's work hard to raise the bar for church leaders.

James Hinkle
January 17, 2011

Editors' Foreword

James is one of those people for whom it is easy to pray the words of Paul: *"I thank my God every time I remember you"* (Philippians 1:3, NIV).

James and his loving wife Harriett have been encouragers and supporters of the work of God wherever they have been. They have sacrificed together to build others up. They love, serve, and give in a way that glorifies God. If all our churches were filled with Jameses and Harrietts, what a blessing it would be.

James wrote this book during his work in ministry. These are not dried-out academic principles that work great *in theory*; these are biblical tools that James has used wherever he has been. Please note that James often wrote in the first person, and his manuscript was developed over several years in various locations.

We appreciate the tireless service and leadership of the Hinkles. With their example in mind, we commend this book to you, and pray that it enables you to be a blessing to your congregation as James has been to ours.

For the glory of Christ!

-The Burns Church of Christ

Chapter 1
The Purpose and Function of Ministry

All Talk, No Action?

"Everyone talks about ministry, but no one does a thing about it." Volumes are written and spoken about the need for effective ministry in this post-modern age. Right-thinking Christians are desirous of being involved in making a difference in their local community.

Involvement in the local church is one of the measures that help members stay. I am reminded of a definition of "football" that was attributed to Vince Lombardi. Coach Lombardi was asked how he would define football. He remarked: "Football is where you have 22 men on the field in desperate need of rest and 60,000 in the stands in dire need of exercise."

The church of today may be a bit like Lombardi's description of football. Most Christians want to be involved in ministry. So why is it so difficult to sustain ministries in the local church? Why do we have to go begging to fill the spots that are necessary to keep a semblance of order in the local body?

There are two reasons for this disease among us. First, we are disobedient to the directions Christ has given us about ministry. Second, we are failing to meet the needs of contemporary society. In this chapter we will deal with the first question leaving the rest of the book to deal with the second.

"What is a minister?"

If we go up to the average member of a church, what answer will we get? Is the answer going to be close to some description of a professional person? Can we detect a minister by the clothes he wears? Are we looking for a person with a certain level of education? One answer we got to this question is, "A minister is a person who is a speaker for all occasions." This minister is one who can make talks at the drop of a hat and he might need to drop his hat on several occasions.

"What is a minister?" Well, everyone knows a minister as a teacher and a preacher. He teaches classes on any and every subject and preaches at least twice each week for the local church. If a crisis arises, he is the first one called and he always knows just what to do in any situation.

"What is a minister?" Here are two answers that show a contrast between the calls to serve. "A minister is one who leads protest marches." "A minister is one who keeps ancient buildings going."

Think long and hard about your own definition. Will it stand the test of Biblical principle? Is it workable in our post-modern society? How does it play out in the church where you worship? What is it like to be a minister in the church that meets in rural Burns, Tennessee or on Broadway in New York?

It is not my purpose to answer every question one might have about ministry but rather to create directions in our thought patterns. Perhaps we can get outside the box of present thinking and attempt to think as we have never thought before. The Bible demands it; the world necessitates it.

Grace-Based Ministry

Let me begin with a broad-scope definition. "One experiences the grace of God then becomes a minister of that grace." *"I became a servant of this gospel by the gift of God's grace given me through the working of his power"* (Ephesians 3:7). Could we begin our quest for dynamic leaders in God's church by looking at this aspect of empowering ministry?

Until we have undergone the humbling, embarrassing business of being washed and cleansed by Jesus, we will remain useless for kingdom work. We can cover land and sea to make a convert to a doctrinal position, and the end result is that he is *"twice as much a son of hell"* as the teacher (Matthew 23:15).

Men judge a message by the life and character of the man who brings it. Until we emphasize that the minister is a person saved by the grace of God, it will be difficult to set the proper example *"in speech, in life, in love, in faith and in purity"* (1 Timothy 4:12). Unless we emphasize the minister's conversion, we will miss the goal of ministry—acting on love *"which comes from a pure heart, a good conscience and a sincere faith"* (1 Timothy 1:5). Persons who have not been touched by God's grace may want to be teachers but *"they do not know what they are talking about or what they so confidently affirm"* (1 Timothy 1:7). They are not ministers of the gospel.

Could it be possible that in some churches, if not most, one can become a church minister without experiencing the grace of God? When you attempt to work out your own salvation without the experience of His amazing grace, it is impossible for Him to work in you to will and to act for his good purpose (Philippians 2:12-13). This statement by Charles Hodge is needed to clarify our understanding of God's grace and how it can affect the modern church: "The doctrine of grace humbles a man without degrading him and exalts him without inflating him."

It might help us in today's church to stop for a moment and make certain that our relationship to Jesus is not that of doctrinal stepchildren but of gracefully and thankfully dear children born and bred at the foot of the cross. The **lifted-up Christ** is necessary for an **uplifting ministry** (John 12:32).

Now for the second broad scope under which I want to work: "Every person is a minister." The New Testament lacks any suggestion that one could possibly be a Christian without being a minister.

The key to understanding this concept is in Paul's use of the metaphor of the **body**. *"Just as each of us has one body with many members, and these members do not all have the same function"* (Romans 12:4). This verse and a lengthy discussion of how a local church works as a body in 1 Corinthians 12 serve as a key ingredient in our quest for ministry. Only by encouraging each part of the body to do its ministry can the body function in keeping with God's purpose. There is a place for the Arnold Schwarzenegger's and the Don Knott's to serve together in harmony and perfect unity. We are to use our gifts in keeping with the grace of God given us (Romans 12:6).

The New Testament lacks any suggestion that one could possibly be a Christian without being a minister.

Ministry Words

By making a careful examination of the cognate words for "ministry" in the New Testament we gain greater insight into the Biblical concept of ministry.

A Bond-Servant

When Peter (1 Peter 2:16) told us to *"live as servants of God,"* he was writing to all Christians. The Greek word for servant is doulos (δουλος). The highest ministry of all is to be a slave to Jesus. I would strongly propose that the attitude of a servant evolves from his being saved by grace. It is only by the constant thankfulness for the eternal grace of God that we can serve effectively as slaves to Christ. Only by humbling ourselves before God can we be lifted up (James 4:10).

A constant sense of being saved by grace allows us to

walk humbly before Him. *"Be completely humble and gentle; be patient, bearing with one another in love"* (Ephesians 4:2).

Being a good slave to Christ is within the reach of every Christian and will lead to a new kind of ministry in the body united. When leaders in God's church begin this new way of thinking about ministry, we may find a new day for the people of God on the earth.

A Worship-Servant

Another word that is used for ministry in the New Testament is *leitourgos*, (λειτουργός) which means servant, minister or worship. We get our modern word "liturgy" from this Greek word. In Acts 13:2, the word is translated as "ministering" by some translations and "worshipping" by others. Worship would be a part of the ministry of the saints. It is used to typify those priests who carried on the "service" in the temple (Luke 1:23).

A Giving Servant

Leitourgia (λειτουργία) is also used in 2 Corinthians 9:12 to denote **giving** of our means to help others. Paul also uses the similar word in Romans 15:27 to point out the need for the Gentiles to minister to their Jewish brothers. Surely no one would argue that the giving ministry is closed to anyone; it is open to all. Even the poor widow of Mark 12:42 can get in on this action. Paul further uses this word for the preaching of the word (Romans15:16). We sometimes apply this concept to the preaching ministry. Even a mundane thing like paying taxes allows government servants to *minister* in their designated areas (Romans 13:6).

A Working Servant

The other word that I have found helpful in this study is the Greek word *diakonos* (διάκονος). This word is used in two senses in Acts 6:1-4. It is used to describe both the preaching of the word by the apostles and the serving of tables by those selected to care for neglected widows. An interesting sidebar in this passage is that the New Testament does not follow our false distinction between the sacred and the secular (Philemon 13; Acts 19:22).

Here are acts of *diakonos* for your study:
- Feeding of hungry people - Acts 6:1
- Feeding of hungry minds - Acts 6:4
- Prayer - Acts 6:4
- Giving - Acts 11:29
- Evangelism - Acts 21:19
- Required personal and evangelistic assistance - Acts 19:22
- The whole life - Acts 20:24

Emil Brunner states: "One thing is supremely important; that all minister, and that nowhere is to be perceived a separation, or even merely a distinction, between those who do and those who do not minister, between the active and the passive members of the body, between those who give and those who receive. There exists in the *ecclessia* a universal duty and right of service, a universal readiness to serve, and at the same time the greatest possible differentiation of functions."

New Testament ministry was a function, not a status

Paul's metaphor of God's people as a **body** shows this distinction between members in their function only and allows for specialized ministries within the body based on gifts and functions but not distinctions of honor within the body. Perhaps Paul has this in mind because, before discussing the distinctions in gifts, he leads with, "*For by the grace of God given to me I say to every one of you: Do not think of yourself more highly that you ought, but rather think of yourself with sober judgment, in accordance with the measure of faith God has given you.*" And he concludes, "*We have different gifts, according to the grace given us*" (Romans 12:3, 6).

Perhaps it would be good to have a more thorough discussion tying the subject of gifts and functions. We can be assured that there are specialized ministries based on gifts and functions, but these are not distinctions of honor within the body (1 Corinthians 12:12-26). This allows us to conclude that New Testament ministry was a function, not a status. Status is always a problem of wrong thinking and Jesus addressed this wrong thinking in Luke 22:25-27.

It might also help us to be clearer if we think of ministering as an action, rather than as a title. In the church, minister is a verb, not a noun! It is not the status of the agent but the nature of the actions which constitutes Christian ministry. It is also the actions of combined body members that will keep the local church on the grow.

Discussion Questions

1. Make a list of things that pop into your mind when the word "minister" is mentioned.

2. Make a list of your own words that mean the same as "minister."

3. Discuss: "Men judge the message by the life and character of the person who brings it."

4. Which biblical word for "ministry" is most meaningful to you? Why?

5. What gifts do you think you have for service in the kingdom?

Chapter 2
Building a Team

From Putting out Fires to Casting Vision

Whether a church is reactive or proactive is determined by the makeup of the members of the team. Some churches are ever in crisis. "Where are we to get the money to continue this program?" "Who will teach this class for the next quarter?" "What can we do about the floundering ministry that has lost all its members?" "Who will lead this group for the new year?"

It gets to be a pattern for churches to always be in crisis. The most faithful are expected to step up to the bat and bail us out again. We worry about them being burned out, but we are frantic about year-end budgets, ministry leaders and filling positions of necessity for an ongoing church. Must leaders always go around putting out fires?

We can look at people not only the way they are now, but how they could be...

Perhaps we need futuristic leaders who look at the local body as what it can be rather than what it is. We can look at people not only the way they are now but how they could be as part of a real team who plan and act as people who are under the direction of the Spirit of peace. The goal is that this church can move toward reaching its full potential as God's family expressing His will for us. By concentrating on team building a church can avoid the tendency to only manage crisis.

Ingredients for a Good Team

What are the ingredients of a good team? Since I do a lot of family counseling, I want to compare the family to a team. What is important to building family can be used to build a good team. In some ways a counselor is like a coach and he tries to bring out the best in all his players. He sends them to the practice field to work on skills that can serve well in the competition that is sure to come. Using some of this family language, I will suggest several things important to team building.

A Sense of Belonging and Love

The first of these is **the sense of belonging and love.** Church growth students have known for a long time that unless members feel like they belong and are loved they will not be active in the local church and will not stick. Without this ingredient, members will hit the church like an egg hits a Teflon skillet and will slide right off to the next church. There are even scales that have been developed to measure a church's "Love-Quotient."

Even the need for social orientation is important for members to stick in a local work. Many people slide right into the front door and right out the back. If people do not feel personally acquainted with at least seven others in the local church, they are highly unlikely to get involved and be a part of a team. Providing opportunities for social interaction can prove "soul-saving" for local churches.

We had this college girl on one of the basketball teams that I coached who was an outstanding ball handler and shooter. She had grown up the inner city of Milwaukee and had played lots of one-on-one with the guys. When we brought her in to play, we were expecting great things of her. The first few practices we knew that we had a problem. She was good and when she got the ball she took it to the hoop and hit a fair share of the buckets.

The real problem was that she had not learned to play as a team. The first game they would just put two people on her and three if that didn't work. Also, her teammates were not willing for her to ball-hog every time and never pass it back to them. We had a problem. Either she would have to learn to play on a team or she would not play at all. She learned to play as a team member and we were able to have a good season, going to the districts and winning two of the three games in the tournament.

Until a team is a team we will not feel that we belong. Our people would like to have the feeling of belonging in the local church. As leaders we must develop a means to coach in a way that creates this personal responsibility for the success of the church. Now if I had all the answers, I would probably still be coaching, but some of you can take this information and run with it. Also, as we develop more on keeping the team going, you might find additional ideas about team building.

A Sense of Purpose and Meaning

The second thing that is important in team building is **a sense of purpose and meaning.** No longer will the stressed out members of this post-modern era involve themselves in something that is not clear in purpose. "Why are we doing this activity?" "Why are we doing it this way?" "What are we accomplishing with this activity?"

How long has it been since leaders in your church have sat down and looked at each program and asked the difficult questions regarding purpose? Not many busy people are going to spend their time and energy keeping a program going just for the sake of keeping it going. It is not the leader's job to keep an activity going long after it has reached its potential and another way can be seen to work better. Many are the programs of local churches that are likened to keeping an ancient building going long after most of the people have ceased coming or just ceased. It is a leader's job to ask those difficult questions of purpose and meaning and be courageous enough to flush the old and have a taste of the new.

I have always heard that industry adopts new ways of doing things first, the government next and schools after them. It is my contention that the church is usually running a mile or two behind them all. Look at the way your sound system is working. Search the times you are meeting. Ask questions about who is coming to what activities.

I'm not advocating radical changes in anything you are now doing. And I am not advocating dilly-dallying with Biblical principles. I am asking that we ask, "Is this activity accomplishing what it is intended to accomplish?" An activity that was effective in the 70s and 80s cannot be resuscitated and brought back on line just because our people are looking for innovative ways of serving in the kingdom. They will not last long where the purpose and meaning are unclear. We are losing some of our best people who use their talents in the business world, but when they come to church they are mildly sedated.

A Sense of Involvement in the Planning

Another principle for team building is **being able to share in the planning.**

Churches are notorious for "Top Down Planning." Leaders work to come up with a good program and ask the church to buy it and do it. I am convinced that many members hear the program presented and applaud the leaders. Then they say "That's a great program. I hope you can accomplish your goals."

Dynamic churches have planning that comes from the bottom up. When the programs are planned by the input of all members, leaders don't have to spend all their time and energy selling it. They don't spend the whole year selling and reselling the program. When members are able to be in on the planning, they will already be involved and the program is theirs.

Churches that want to get more people involved must

take the time to lead in planning that involves the people in all stages of development. If it is *our* program and not *their* program, we are already committed to it. Only a few groups of leaders have the clout to present a program from the top that will be sustained throughout the year. These leaders are so few and far between that it would seem that most of us could use a little team approach to local church work.

It is not true that we can do anything we set our hearts on. In my basketball playing days I was a point guard. My greatest height was five feet and eleven inches. I could never play center for the Chicago Bulls no matter how much desire I had.

A Sense of Expectations

In building a team it is important to have the right people in the right positions and that all players **have a clear understanding of what is expected of them.** Whatever team sport we can name, the players must know what their position is and what is expected of each player. One block on a football team will not get the ball forward but each player doing his work can move the team toward its goal. One screen at the right time can free a player for a three-pointer but the other players must be in their positions to accomplish the goal.

"We need a teacher for the third grade. The teacher who has been teaching this class for the last forty years has just died. She was such a jewel. Could you go in the class and see what you can do. Let us know if you need anything." How's that for clear understanding?

Make a list of questions that this new teacher might need answered if she is to feel confident about the new assignment. Then we might want to go back and revise our way of getting team members. Why are we surprised that some of our most dedicated members are not accepting assignments and staying involved until "death do we part?"

Compare this to an education ministry that has

involvement at all levels in their program. They have sat down with each teacher and carefully written job descriptions for each class. They have established an integrated system for new teachers and have an ongoing teacher training program in operation. When these new people are asked to help, they are accepted as part of a team and they are clear in what it is that a third grade teacher does.

Dennis Williams and Kenneth Gangel have written a helpful book: *Volunteers for Today's Church: How To Recruit and Retain Workers*. There are other books on the market that might give us a few good ideas. Leaders who want to build a good team must spend time with each ministry, clarifying just what is expected of each team member.

A Sense of Genuine Responsibility

How important do our team members feel? **An experience of genuine responsibility** is the next ingredient of team building. As I have stated earlier, there is little motivation for modern church goers to keep ancient buildings going. Busy-for-busy-sake will not go very far in this time starved generation.

A tell-tale need of a modern churchgoer is the desire to make a difference.

One of the tell-tale needs of the modern churchgoer is the desire to make a difference. If we are going to be involved, it has to be in an area where we can make a difference. If that is not made abundantly clear, the team will lose its best players. Clear job descriptions and careful bottom-up planning can help each feel genuine responsibility for the assignment and the task.

A Sense of Achievement

All of these work in unison to develop **a sense of achievement.** Life is too short for us to be involved in meaningless activity. Many church members are involved in service clubs, community and school projects and feel that they are accomplishing things for their community. When we ask for the same commitment for the work in the local church, we get a dull excuse that says there is no room for another time-consuming activity. Might it be that they just haven't seen the local ministry as having the potential of great achievement? Any family member who does not stay involved in the family activity is casting a vote for their sense of nonsense that the church is asking them to participate in. There is little question that the modern Christian is over involved. The question is why are they not spending that energy in the ministry of the local church?

How much do the team members know about the on-going working of all team members. Each week during football season, a battery of coaches will sit for hours developing game plans. During practice they will inform all the players of each cog in the wheel for victory. Each player knows the plan and how he or she fits into this week's game.

Now as we move to the local church, what is happening? If there is a game plan it usually stays in the minds of leaders and is not discussed in detail with each member. There is a quarterly meeting and a yearly directive but where is the week-by-week planning for the ministry? One of the grievous sins of modern leadership is non-communication.

A Sense of Inclusion and Information

Our ministry leaders meet with the "board of elders" quarterly. They are asked to come in to a meeting and give a report and seek approval for any new activities. This may be a good step in the right direction, but where is the working out of the game plan? Where does the real plan develop? Is it communicated well to all team members? Are some teams duplicating the work of other teams? When the game is being played are there two people running out in the same formation? Openness is good but continual planning and working together with all team members can get some plans made that can accomplish great things for the Lord. **A desire**

to be kept informed is of utmost importance if the team is going to accomplish its goals.

A Sense of Recognition

One of my heroes in church building was the late Ira North. I visited the Madison Church in Nashville during Ira's apex as a church builder. During the service he marched several people to the pulpit and asked others to stand as he noted the activities and ministries they were involved in. I thought at the time that this was a great way to keep the church informed of the good that they were doing. Later I recognized that this was a powerful motivator. **A desire for recognition** is a key ingredient in team building. Ira understood what many church leaders failed to fathom.

It is not so much that a person seeks recognition for the work of ministry, but that the need for recognition is built deep within by God himself. Letting our light shine before men is not done for selfish reasons but to glorify God by what is done. Paul once wrote, *"I commend to you our sister Phoebe, a servant of the church in Cenchreae"* (Romans 16:1). Read the rest of Romans 16 and become aware that there is great motivation when we give proper recognition to those who *"serve one another in love"* (Galatians 5:13). Paul also wrote *"The elders who direct the affairs of the church well are worthy of double honor"* (1 Timothy 5:17).

A Sense of Security

A final ingredient in the well-being of the family and team is **a reasonable degree of security.** Here I'm not talking about secure buildings and grounds. Here is where the philosophy of the church comes into being. Performance is not the basis of our relationships in Christ or in his church. We are loved unconditionally by our awesome God and we are to let that unconditional love permeate every portal of God's building. There can be no security when the local church practices works salvation. Somehow after we are saved by grace, the fungus of performance creeps back in and we lose any security because performance can never be perfect.

Unconditional love is our security blanket from which comes the feeling that we are accepted as we are in the local church. Motivation by guilt is cast far from us, and we serve a risen Savior with grateful hearts and lives full of praise. Feeling accepted and secure in our relationships in the local family can lead to loving, productive service to the King.

By studying Figure 2-1 leaders can learn to motivate by using this as a grid. Go from lower left in a clockwise direction to the lower right. The more leaders are willing to self-disclose and share who they really are the more trust they receive. Trust is continually fostered by communication. When this happens there is motivation for the team to do its best.

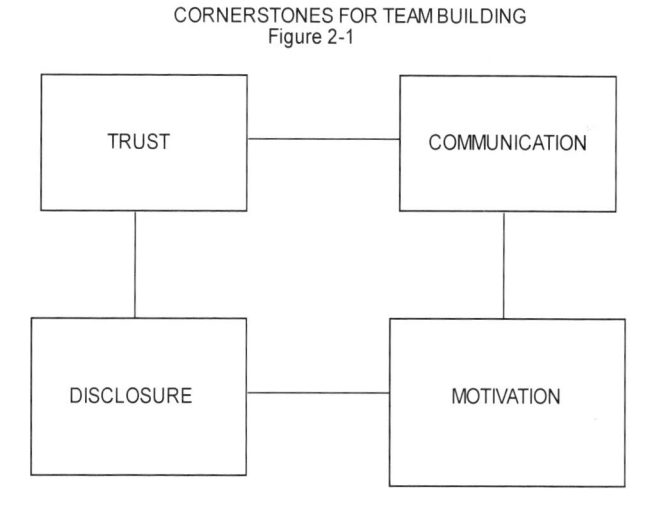

CORNERSTONES FOR TEAM BUILDING
Figure 2-1

TRUST	COMMUNICATION
DISCLOSURE	MOTIVATION

For your additional study, "The Ten Commandments of Team Building" by Robert Dale might stimulate further discussion:
    1. Develop personal ownership of your team's life and work. People support what they help create.
    2. Surface expectations. Everybody expects

something from the group they take part in.
3. Create a "we" climate. A family atmosphere depends on a sense of kinship.
4. Recognize relational roles in teams.
5. Do team repair.
6. Define the core mission of your organization.
7. Define the core task groups you work with.
8. Develop team task descriptions.
9. Monitor task roles on your team.
10. Learn to manage meetings.

Discussion Questions

1. What experiences have you had with a team? At work? At play? While volunteering?

2. Which of the characteristics of team building mean the most to you? Explain your answer.

3. How can you help to build the team in your church?

4. Study Figure 2-1. How does this work in your life?

5. Which of the Ten Commandments by Robert Dale mean the most to you? Why?

Chapter 3
The What and Why of Team Building

A Learned Skill: The "What"

When a local leadership decides to build a team and really gets serious about it, it is then time to ask the questions that we all wanted to ask but were afraid of the answers we might get.

If the leader has the gift of leadership, "*let him govern diligently*" (Romans 12:8). But does that mean that leaders have a gift for forging members into a good team where all players feel they belong and are contributing to the team's success?

I would begin this chapter with the proposition that team building is a learned skill. To me basketball was a natural skill. Having grown up with eight brothers and lots of cousins, I discovered that basketball was natural for me. I knew what to do with the ball and how to get the pass to the right person for the score. When I attempted to teach this to my team members, I failed miserably. I found out very soon that doing something yourself and teaching others to do it do not require the same skills. New and different skills are required if a leader is to mold diverse people with differing gifts into a team.

However, I found that with a lot of work, one can acquire the skills necessary to team build. But it is a learned skill. It took a lot of studying the techniques of other coaches to get through to me. I looked for models who were able to get men and women from all walks of life to function as a team. I read books from coaches, viewed videos, and watched them in practice. Before long I had learned the skills to form a team.

Learn from the Masters

By studying the writings of masters, attending seminars and listening to tapes and viewing videos, we can learn much about what it takes to build teams in the local church. One of the practical requirements at Fuller Seminary is that ministry students in their programs study churches that have formed good teams and learn how it was done. Since team building is a learned skill, we can study good models and learn to build good teams.

Team building is critical to success. Whether we are talking about a sport or a church, unless we develop a team, we are doomed to failure or mediocrity. Without the team spirit the local body will fracture and move in directions that are more personal than godly.

There is no success in the local church when it fails to be a body with all members functioning in their gifted capacities. There is nothing more critical to success than team building. The time leaders spend in molding the team together is the best time that can be spent. Never tire of building the team for the lasting progress for the season. Long-term accomplishment is dependent on the leaders' success in this crucial area.

The Fun of Team Building

Do not look at this effort at team building as pure drudgery. In fact, the efforts that we can put forth at team building can be **fun**. It is more fun to coach a team than to have to concentrate on several agendas and have to manage the crises that arise.

We should enjoy our work in the kingdom. Looking at the work of God as boring or depressing means we have lost our joy of serving. Many have allowed this joy to seep out as the team has disintegrated. How many head coaches have lost enthusiasm for the game and have been sent packing because they were not able to get their team to be a team? How many leaders have been sent on their way before their time because they have been unable to form a team where peace and harmony prevail?

The Frustration of Team Building

I would be remiss if I did not add a sub-point to the point of fun. Not only can team building be fun, it can be **frustrating**. To see the potential of a local body and not be able to move it in the direction of a team can so frustrate us that we are ready to apply for our license to sell insurance. Many churches are sleeping giants. They have the gifts, the talents, and the potential for becoming a power in the community and the world. For some reason they remain a sleeping giant for years. A new leader comes and tries in vain to awaken this giant but he leaves in frustration after a few years.

Many churches are sleeping giants.

No matter what is attempted the same result remains. Team building can be frustrating, but that does not mean that we should stop trying. Learning to build a team can move from frustration to fun if we learn the lesson well and start being coaches rather than Monday morning quarterbacks.

The Reward of Team Building

Before I leave this area entirely, I would like to add that team building can be fabulously **rewarding**. No longer do the leaders have to do all the work. The team functions and the church builds itself up in love. Leaders can look with satisfaction when the local church operates as a team. For years into the future leaders can work with satisfaction as the team is maintained and operating efficiently. Sure there will be some creaks and groans, but the overall satisfaction will be

He only expects us to be faithful to the trust He has given us. *"Now it is required that those who have been given a trust must prove faithful"* (1 Corinthians 4:2). When we quit waiting for Michael Jordan to appear and start working with the players we have, we will truly make progress.

Sometimes leaders are a bit disgusted with the sheep. But they are the only sheep we have. We either love them or lose them. Dr. Lynn Anderson wrote a book a few years back on shepherding called *They Smell Like Sheep*. As I was writing this section, I came across a note from Bill Gates, in his book *Business @ the Speed of Thought*. He writes:

> "A good e-mail system ensures that bad news travels fast, but your people have to be willing to send the news. You have to be constantly receptive to bad news, and then you have to act on it. Sometimes I think my most important job as CEO is to listen for bad news. If you don't act on it, your people will eventually stop bringing bad news to your attention. And that's the beginning of the end."

The willingness to hear hard truth is vital not only for CEOs of big corporations but also for anyone who loves the truth. Sometimes the truth sounds like bad news, but it is just what we need.

Living in fantasy land is a Disney World Adventure, but it will only debilitate the local team. Learning to work with the people the Lord has given us may be frustrating, but it can be rewarding. *"It is required in stewards, that a man be found faithful"* (1 Corinthians 4:2, KJV).

Because Every Part Matters

The second idea that needs expressing under the heading of Team: Each team contains all body parts. Paul argues in 1 Corinthians that the local church is the body of Christ. *"The body is a unit, though it is made up of many parts; and though all its parts are many, they form one body"* (1 Corinthians 12:12).

One of the most painful injuries I ever had in playing basketball was a jammed finger. I actually broke my little pinky finger on my right hand. It is still larger at the knuckle than it should be. While it was mending (it never healed), I was careful to keep it protected. If I was playing basketball, I would tape it to the finger next to it. In this way it would never come in contact with the ball. The other finger protected it until it became less sensitive.

Yet it was still a part of the body. It remains to this day a part of the body. We sometimes forget that even members that hurt and struggle are still members of the team. We don't take a vote and see who will survive. We either survive as a body, or the whole thing heads for the cemetery.

We may give honor to the starters on the team, but the rest of the body parts are necessary to the proper functioning of the whole. If they were all one part, where would the body be? Each body part contributes to the whole. Each local church contains all the body parts necessary for a church to function. That means that we could do a much better job of helping each part to feel and function as a member of this local body. Spending time looking for superstars is a waste of time; furthermore it will cause us to overlook and not work with those that are already on board. A team contains all the players necessary to play the game, but each team leader must remember that the team contains all the body parts to function in the game. I didn't say that every team can win every game it plays, but in the body, God's grace will assure us of the victory. *"This is the victory that has overcome the world, even our faith"* (1 John 5:4).

Because it Prevents Burnout

"Two are better than one, because they have a good return for their labor. If either of them falls down, one can help the other up. But pity anyone who falls and has no one to help them up." This quote from Ecclesiastes 4:9-10 will help us to understand the necessity of being a team. I am convinced that one of the things that causes more people to leave the ministry or just to get discouraged is **burnout**. Being on a team can help prevent

burnout.

Do you as a leader see yourself as an active power in your church? Do you feel that you are a spiritual leader? Do you think of yourself as a dynamic entity? If you do, you have not reached the danger zone in the world of burnout.

It is important that I write a few words on this often-talked-about malady in Christian circles. I have felt it myself and have counseled many who have wrestled with the burnout syndrome. All I can do here is to suggest some of the causes and let you know that you as a leader must deal with burnout in yourself and then you can deal with it in your local leaders.

The first cause of burnout in leadership is family problems. The Devil can throw more discouragements with family problems than most leaderships can handle. Any time we have family problems, we will feel the pale horse of burnout riding in our direction. Building strong families is the sought-after goal of most leaders, but reality sets in and discouragement comes in hot and heavy. The people who are the most dedicated are the ones who will suffer the most disastrous fate when it comes to burnout.

An elder who had served for years moved out of his house and left the church. He had gotten so involved with another woman that he was willing to follow this emotional trail to its grievous end. That can make a whole church feel the pain of burnout. There are churches that never recover from such a debacle.

The team spirit could help us work through family problems that devastate church and leaders. More involvement with people on a daily basis might help us to spot the problem earlier and take practice sessions to deal with this flaw in one of our team members. Through the course of several disciplined practice sessions, deadly destructive life directions can be changed.

Anyone who has been around very long can tell us about the burnout that can come when there are financial problems. Even though things may be changing for the better, it is still difficult to find a family that has properly managed its money. It is like a team where all the resources must be put to proper use. The tall and the short must be taught their proper function. It is not the amount of money that we make that is most important. It is the way we manage our money.

Would it be possible to have training seminars for all of our families in the art of money management? When I was a coach, I had to teach my players how to manage their time so their grades would meet the qualifications for eligibility. Leaders can find ways to help themselves and their flock to manage funds. When the creditors are calling and the pressure is on for us to pay up and we have come to the end of our money before the end of the month, we are a prime candidate for burnout. Good work in this area can pay great dividends in the future. If we are one of those pietistic individuals who cannot be bothered by such mundane things as filthy lucre, there is little to be done but let the natural consequences kick us in the rear. For the rest it's a good idea to spend our money on paper before we actually shell it out. God expects us to tell our money what to do and not vice versa.

Because it Strengthens Each of Us

Another area that must be examined carefully is the matter of an uncooperative spirit in those with whom we work. There are always a few who seem bent on going their own direction without any thought to the need for team effort. The "ball-hog" who thinks that his way is the only way for playing the game will lead to frustration and despair.

When we come up with a sure cure for all the ills of the church and community and those with whom we work can't seem to feel it as we do, we can become discouraged; then burnout is hiding around the next corner. One of the things that I was taught in the early days of my training was that we must be careful not to get our egos tied to a pet project. It took lots of years and hard knocks to implant this lesson in me. Many are still learning this lesson, and the quicker we learn it the less burnout will show in our ministry. Using the "bottom-up" approach to leadership will help us avoid some of the headaches that accompany uncooperativeness in the brothers and sisters we are called to lead.

One of the most difficult things that we have to deal with is criticism. I can't name the times that a good brother or sister has come to me with a little "constructive" criticism that left me totally destroyed. I like the way Billy Graham once answered the question about how he dealt with critics. He said that he looked carefully at the criticism, and if the comment had validity he would make necessary corrections. If the criticism was just sour grapes, he would write the critic's name on a golf ball. It was surprising how much that helped his drives. Charles Spurgeon once wrote: "Get a friend to tell you your faults, or better still, welcome an enemy who will watch you keenly and sting you savagely. What a blessing such an irritating critic will be to a wise man, what an intolerable nuisance to a fool."

We all know that leaders will receive criticism. Yet, this knowledge doesn't prevent us from going into conflict. I learned several years ago something that has been helpful to me. Almost all conflict that is inward comes when our role is challenged. That means that when someone criticizes our leadership, sermon, class, family, or other area where our role is in jeopardy, it is easy for us to go into conflict. (See Newton Malony's book *When Getting Along Seems Impossible* for a lengthy discussion of this subject.)

There are two truths that we must keep constantly before us: 1) God made us and 2) God loves us. When we hang our hats on these two truths, we can function effectively and avoid the smashing of our motivation and falling into the pit of burnout.

Because of Synergy

There is one last reason to team build that I want to share in this chapter. I don't know who coined the word **Synergy**, but it's a good word to describe the effort of a team. The basic definition of "synergy" is "the whole is greater than the sum of its parts." The concept is as old as nature itself. The apostle Paul certainly gave the concept precedence 1 Corinthians 12. The body is a good example of synergy. When we have equal concern for each other, we harness a power greater than the Lone Ranger by himself.

Effective churches will work toward building a good team. In any good team even the water boy is valued. When each part is given proper recognition and honor, a church can be a light in the dark world as it serves together to enter the winner's circle with Jesus and be crowned with the laurel of victory.

Discussion Questions

1. Do you agree or disagree with the statement: "When members work as individuals, the activities of the church will splinter"? Explain your answer.

2. Read again the statement by Bill Gates. What is your response to what he says?

3. How could your church teach money management?

4. What experiences have you had with burnout? Share one story.

5. What is the most fun part of team building?

Chapter 4
Good Team, Bad Team

We can always tell a good team from a bad team, or can we? Ministry is not as precise as the score at the end of the game. Also, it is God who keeps the final score and judgment is above, and not from man. The final tally is in His hands and He alone knows the destiny of all of us. It's not over till it's over; however, it could prove helpful to look at a series of contrasts between a good and bad team. I'm sure I am borrowing from some great writer but at the time I didn't reference notes I made several years ago and am unable to find these points so I can give the proper credit.

Team Agenda vs. Personal Agenda

Contrast One: Team agenda versus personal agenda. I once had the opportunity to visit "Speakers' Corner" in Saint James Park, London. There were a number of people who had their soap boxes and were having a go at persuading others to accept whatever ideology they had on their agenda at the moment.

Having an agenda for a business meeting is fine and dandy. Having thirteen agendas is not okay. A meeting with thirteen agendas is the difference between a bad and a good team. When a local church is working as a team, all are going in the same direction. When a church is having difficulty, each member "jumps on a horse and rides off in all directions."

The *we* versus *they* attitude is a common phenomenon in local churches when personal agendas are allowed to run rampant. Our language betrays us. How do we look at the ministries of our local body? Are they having an activity, or are we having an activity? Are they involved in a project or are we involved in a project? The lack of team agenda can habitually hamper the goals of the group and cause competition between lighthouses.

John Maxwell defines servant leadership in the following five points in his book, *The 21 Indispensable Qualities of a Leader*.

- A leader puts others ahead of his own agenda. The servant leader is intentionally aware of his people's needs, available to help them, and able to accept their desires as important.
- A leader possesses the confidence to serve. Servanthood and security are inseparable. How we treat those who follow us is really a reflection of the way we think about ourselves. Someone who says that he is too important to serve is battling feelings of insecurity.
- A leader initiates service to others. Great leaders seize the opportunity to serve without expecting anything in return.
- A leader is not position conscious. Servant leaders do not focus on position or rank.
- A leader serves out of love. True service in the kingdom is not motivated by manipulation or self-promotion. A leader's influence depends on the depth of his concern for others.

Interdependent vs. Independent vs. Overdependent

Contrast Two: Interdependent versus independent or over-dependent. Here I think of a screen pass in football. The blockers attempt a block, quickly release, and then the receiver falls in behind these blockers, and the receiver is on his way. All of this works fine if every man does his work. There is an interdependence going on during this play and probably every play. If one man or several decide that they want to block in their own way and place and forget to work together, the play will lose ground. The independent spirit is what made America great, but it is the independent spirit that chooses to work together for the greater good that is worth writing home about.

I contend that the language of church has changed. We now use consumer language in our interactions in the family of God. Some of our conversations in church sound a lot like someone explaining why he wants to trade cars, sell a house, or get rid of some old clothes.

I understand that people can get genuinely distressed about personal dissatisfactions in their relationships in a local church. But many of these reasons often come down to the sense that my needs are not being met, and other members are not doing an adequate job of meeting those needs.

I believe in the advocating of self in personal relationships in the local body. Each person has a genuine human need to be treated with love, fairness, and respect. Being a patsy for some Diotrephes who wants to manipulate and control is not good for oneself or the church. When others try to control what you feel or think, it is time to assert your boundaries. It is not right to remain silent when treated unfairly, and it is right to confront and expect others to follow agreed-on responsibilities.

But here danger lurks when I focus mainly on my needs and the failure of others to meet them. When I confuse my desires with my needs, when I confuse behavior that is totally unacceptable (like the list in Galatians 5:19ff) and behavior that bothers me or saddens me (such as not receiving enough love, support, and interest and not doing what I want when I want it), I have become a consumer. The consumer attitude turns church disappointment into church fights and tragedies, and attitude negates constructive efforts for improvement that lead to constructive change.

Consumer thinking insinuates itself in a number of different ways. The first way is reflected in the conclusion that it's about as good as it's going to get. The deficiency in our brother is not going to go away. The moods in our brothers are here to stay. Attitudes that we would like to change are not going to change. Opinions are digging in and singing the song "I shall not be moved." Obsessions and compulsions are not likely to diminish. The local church may never give the euphoria of hanging from the chandeliers.

The second way consumerism flexes its muscle emerges right after a seminar or workshop on some area of body life. We awake the next morning all enthusiastic about the new church and new attitudes. This new approach will surely shape up the local church. Positive changes are in the making. It is hard to accept that the negatives in this relationship are not going to take the wings of morning and fly to the uttermost parts of the world. Even if I work hard to be a part of the solution rather than a part of the problem, the knowledge that there are certain parts of the body which will continue to creak and let me down is ever before me.

Working on ingrained problems is a long-range goal of effective leadership. What we do in education and relationships can make a great difference in what happens in a local church. But to expect that all the flaws and painful parts of a hospital for sinners will disappear, is to expect what the Holy Scriptures never promised. The core strengths and core weaknesses will always be with us. The trick is to build on the strengths and contain and soften the impact of the negatives when they exert themselves.

The next way that consumer thinking can invade the local church is in the manner of comparison. In the consumer model we are always looking for a newer and better model. The economies of our world are based on comparisons between the good and the better. Pentium II is not enough, upgrade! Who cares if what I have is adequate, upgrade! The consumer model makes comparison with your church and others a daily challenge.

This happens especially if you get a bit peeved with local directions, ministries, or leaders. You may have no intention of changing churches, but the deadly virus of "comparisionitus" is an insidious and diabolical one. Members can obsess about these comparisons and create enough dissension in a local church to bring on an Excedrin Headache Number Five. We have no idea what the other church is like or whether, over the long haul, it will meet my consumer needs.

Here is a little test taken from William Doherty in *Take Back Your Marriage* and adapted to the local church rather than marriage.

Consumer Church Quiz

Is your attitude toward your church consumer-oriented?

Circle your answer in the questions below:

1. I *(often, sometimes, rarely)* compare my church unfavorably with other churches.

2. In relation to our problems, I *(often, sometimes, rarely)* dwell on my church's deficiencies; not on my own.

3. I *(often, sometimes, rarely)* concentrate on how my church is not meeting my needs rather than on how I am not meeting my church's needs.

4. I *(often, sometimes, rarely)* keep score: I add up when I do good things or when I think my church does something bad.

5. I *(often, sometimes, rarely)* think my church is getting a better deal in this relationship than I am.

6. I *(often, sometimes, rarely)* focus on my church's defects rather than on its strengths.

7. I *(often, sometimes, rarely)* wonder if I should hold out for a better church rather than the one I presently have.

8. When we have hard times, I *(often, sometimes, rarely)* ask myself whether the effort I'm putting in with this church is worth it.

Enter the total number of times you used each answer:
Often: _____   Sometimes: _____   Rarely: _____

If most of your answers are "rarely," you are not treating your church like a car that you are trading because it has rust. If most of your answers are "sometimes," ask yourself if the things that you want are disguising themselves as things you absolutely need. If three or more of your answers are "often," consumerism has severely infected your view of church. Do you wish to be a member of the body or take a tourist visa to travel the way of fantasy?

Distinguishing core needs from optional wants is central to resisting consumerism. The best way to keep the consumer culture from dominating your relationship is to see yourself as a vital member of the team in a local church. That means you must be intentional and committed in your dedication to the local brotherhood of believers. Being a team member means that I take responsibility to make things better and to value the relationship above my own personal interest. *"Do nothing out of selfish ambition or vain deceit, but in humility consider others better than yourselves"* (Philippians 2:3).

Sense of Purpose vs. Just a Job

Contrast Three: Sense of Purpose versus Just a Job. It is no easy task to get team members to see the need for what they are doing and not get bogged down in the minutiae of the job. Few leaders have an overall picture of the way the church works, so it is understandable that members come to the task with a view to doing a job, not accomplishing a purpose.

It makes for good coaching when we can get the purpose of the task clearly in the mind of the player. I was working with my basketball team in the earlier part of the year and our main purpose was conditioning. Instead of having the girls run laps around the gym in a somewhat straight line, I asked them to run the laps following the lines on the gym floor. Now if you have ever seen a gym floor, you will know that there are lines going in all directions. By running the lines, the player can build up ankle and knee muscles. The first time they tried it, they were wondering "what was the purpose." After they saw the purpose, they were looking at it as a challenge, not a job.

Self Starters vs. Sitters and Waiters

Contrast Four: Self-starters versus wait to be told. Some churches have sent self-starters to an early grave. These self-starters have enthusiastically suggested new ministries and have been shot from the saddle. Now they are sitting around waiting to be told what to do, where to do it, and when. Good team members are quickly turned into bad team members or just turned out. There are many dynamic leaders who have left churches that stymied their creativity and have become great leaders in other churches that recognized and used their gifts. Some of us sit back and wish we had that kind of team member with us and we can't figure it out.

The paradigm for some churches that use the top-down approach is what keeps many members from becoming active servants in the local church. Many are sitting around waiting to be told what to do, where to do it, and when. Without a change of paradigm, it will be difficult for churches to use self-starters in the ways God has gifted them. When church leaders are walking around Gerber-feeding the flock, is there any wonder that the church is made up of a lot of crying infants?

Innovative vs. Conservative

Contrast Five: Innovative versus conservative, traditional and stodgy. This could be a sub-point to the last contrast, but I wanted to list it as having separate value. Churches grew in the fifties and sixties. They were creating new paradigms and new methods of reaching the lost. Church leaders were willing to accept the criticism of others as they experimented with new, creative ways of reaching the lost. These methods became set in concrete, and are now perceived as the only ways of getting the job done.

Churches that are asking difficult questions about how to reach the lost in this post-modern age are the ones who are turning the world right-side up in today's challenging environment. The parable of the new wine in old wineskins has a modern-day application. It is easy for us to sit in our comfort zones and declare, "The old is better" (Luke 5:37-39).

How are we to meet the needs of modern man? Is the old really better? Why has Christianity not become a more vital commodity in our present age? Is it because we are not interested in sharing the gospel, or is it that we are stuck in modes of the past that have not allowed the light of the love of God to shine through?

Bad teams never learn any new plays. They never take the old play book and revise it or throw it away and start anew. The gospel never changes, but the play book needs a new page or two or three or more. If the opposer knows all our plays, he can certainly shut down any gain that we can make. Winners for God are creative and innovative.

Helping Hands vs. "Not My Job"

Contrast six: Good teams support each other; bad teams say "it's not my job." Wrestling may work out as an individual sport. Try individualism in soccer, and it won't work. You're either a part of the team or you sit on the bench.

When a good team takes the field, you know if it is bad or

good by the amount of participation of each team member. When a church is on the field, you can tell if it's good or bad by the quality and quantity of participation. When half the church is in danger of burnout, and the other half behaves like couch potatoes, you have a form of inequity that leads you into survival mode. I read the results of a study several years ago that was attempting to determine why there was so little participation in the church by the thirty-something's. Career and child rearing seemed the logical answer. The survey found that it was more a disease called burnout. It seems that all these good people were superstars in their twenties and early thirties. Then they began to withdraw in phenomenal numbers.

The study showed that many came back again for involvement in the late forties. Those who were earlier involved to the nth degree backed away from work and waited until they got over what ailed them.

Why do we have to lose the most productive workers during their most productive time? We don't! Developing a good team means that leaders make sure that there is ample support for all workers and that none feel that they are doing it alone. Support from all leaders and from all members can come if leaders allow the church to take responsibility for the growth of the local body.

Not only is there a great need for recognition and help in vital areas, but a good team is always looking for ways to support those who are at the helm and those who are carrying on the little tasks that make for a good church. Bad teams are always critical instead of encouraging. Bad teams are like Monday Morning quarterbacks. They know all the best plays that should have been called, and they don't mind voicing their opinions loud and clear. Does it sometimes remind you of a sports talk show that allows callers to voice their opinions about everything from the coach to the water boy? Churches have a lot of people in the bleachers yelling at the top of their voices. It reminds me a bit of the lady whose car had stalled in the intersection. Some guy three cars back was sitting on his horn. Finally, in desperation, she went back and calmly asked, "If you would kindly go and start my car, I will be happy to sit here and blow your horn."

Is it true that the people who are hard at work in the local church don't have time to throw bricks? Ira North used the statement that I have always remembered: "A horse can't pull while he is kicking and can't kick while he is pulling." Good teams win or lose together. Bad teams say, "It's not my job." They also say loudly and obnoxiously, "You are not doing it right!" As the late Ira North often said, "I like the way we are doing it better than the way you're not doing it."

This leads to a participative philosophy as opposed to the autocratic approach to leadership. I will have some other things to say about this in a later chapter.

Enjoy vs. Irritate

Contrast seven: Good teams enjoy their co-workers; bad teams tolerate co-workers. For those who are involved in a ministry that is in their gifted area and for which they have received some appreciation, ministry is fun, not drudgery. You can feel it when you walk into the room, church, class, group, or family. They like each other and would give their best to see that all get involved and enjoy the activities. Joy is found in abundance in all the activities of a dynamic church.

The spirit of joy pervades the worship assembly. You can feel it when Christians meet for church and when they meet at the grocery store. Good churches spend a lot of time together in non-church activities. The church that plays together stays together.

It's the spirit of workers that I want to see bolstered. To want to bask in the feeling of what I am doing makes a difference and that others of like mind are on the team because they like to be there brings a sense of joy that works deeply into our inner person. I want to help the church be a joy-full place where people love to come and bring their friends.

Thriving on Adventure vs. Running from Risks

Contrast eight: A good team thrives on a challenge; a bad team avoids risks. The same old thing is still the same old thing. The old is still looked on as better. There is security in the old, and rocking the boat is not to be tolerated.

Churches reach a comfort zone and are satisfied to remain there. Any attempt at harnessing the power of creative and innovative people will be lost in the shuffle. Most of the better people will shuffle right out the back door.

It is risky to become a Christian, and it should be risky to remain an active one. Satan can lull us to sleep. We start to feel like we have arrived, and we sit down on do nothing and lean back on do less. Paul may have been quoting the words of an ancient Christian hymn in Ephesians 5:14. It would be interesting to go back to that ancient church and participate in the singing of, *"Wake up, O sleeper, rise from the dead, and Christ will shine on you."* It might be that we could sing this hymn to the profit of the modern church.

Avoiding risks can keep the fearful at home on Sunday and Monday and Tuesday. Fear can stymie the activity of a phobic person and a phobic church. When all is said and done, there is more said than done. John says that *"Perfect love drives out fear,"* (1 John 4:18) and we need all the love we can get. Good teams are not afraid to take risks. Bad teams relish the status quo. Good teams are not afraid to try, because they are not afraid to fail. New programs can begin and if they don't work out, the good team will go back to the drawing board and try again. Bad teams would fear failure, and therefore they are sure to fail. The surest way to fail is to fail to try. Good teams try lots of new things and flush those that don't work and keep working and reworking those that do.

Those teams that thrive on challenge have a sense of urgency. Teams that avoid risks are never in a hurry. The virtue of patience goes to seed and what is looked upon as patience is really laziness. Good teams develop a sense of ownership while bad teams just put in time.

These eight contrasts point out the need for leadership that seeks change and improvement rather than a leadership that is digging its heels in and resisting change. The desired leadership seeks change not just for change sake, but change that is built firmly on revealed truth and modern application of that truth. We must never attempt to change anything before firmly deciding what things can never be changed.

Discussion Questions

1. Discuss "personal agendas" and how they work in a local church.

2. Which of the points by John Maxwell makes the most sense to you? Why?

3. How can "consumer language" become a detriment to serving others?

4. How did you do on the consumer-driven church quiz? What did you learn?

5. Of the eight contrasts in this chapter, which made you the most uncomfortable? Explain.

Chapter 5
Finding the Real Disease

Making the Diagnosis

During the discourse on the Mount, Jesus warned about the "eye of the body." *"The eye is the lamp of the body. If your eyes are good, your whole body will be full of light. But if your eyes are bad, your whole body will be full of darkness. If then the light within you is darkness, how great is that darkness"* (Matthew 6:22-23).

The eye is the window of the soul. In childlike simplicity, Jesus lets us know that the heart is capable of both good and bad, light and darkness. The state of a window is the determining factor about the amount of light that passes through. My wife can spot a smudge a block away. I have been in houses with windows that were completely shut off from the sunlight. What a dismal and dark existence.

When we go to the doctor, he will often look into the eyes. Something in them must tell the doctor that something is wrong inside those windows. Might it be so with a church?

The patient is pale and feverish. She is anemic in attendance. *"For this cause many among you are weak and sickly, and not a few sleep"* (1 Corinthians 11:30, ASV). There are infective factions that are running rampant through the very blood stream of the body. Spastic movements of leaders are making everyone wonder if there is a clear direction for the local body. Some may be financially exhausted.

When there is a feeling of frustration in the local body, members will have a "feeling" that something is not right. It is similar to those hard-to-describe physical feelings…a shortness of breath, shooting pain, a sense of unease…that we feel from time to time but can't explain.

You can notice it in the local church when the leaders and followers are wringing their hands and wondering why things are not moving as they once did. People are leaving, and teachers are harder to find and servers are disappearing faster than we can recruit. If your eyes are bad, the whole body is full of darkness.

Doctor, can this church be healed?

Looking Beyond the Symptoms

A good doctor listens to the patient's complaint. He runs the tests, and he looks beyond the first complaint to find the real problem. First answers are usually wrong. It might have been that in the past doctrinal errors could have been the diagnoses. Today, conservative churches are dying, and conservative churches are growing. Today, liberal churches are dying and liberal churches are growing. The real problem with the eyes still remains for us to identify and make the correction.

We don't want to treat a brain tumor with an aspirin, or a bleeding ulcer with an antacid. What are the symptoms? What is the disease? What is the presenting problem? Is the pain in the stomach or the back?

Let's look at five symptoms to see if the patient's condition is terminal. We must be careful not to react too quickly before the final tests are read and deciphered. We might have to call in a specialist.

Symptom One: Nothing but Self-Interest

In a recent education supervisors' meeting I heard two explanations about the teacher shortage. One person said that it was difficult to get teachers because other classes serve coffee and donuts and they didn't want to give this up. Another made a quick diagnosis that some would not teach because this was the only time that they saw their friends in the other Bible classes.

There is **a malady of selfishness** that has invaded our society and has been found to have diseased the church. It is the epidemic of selfishness that can cause a body to see only darkness. It is easy for us in this modern age to serve ourselves at the expense of others.

Dying to self is not an easy thing to do in any age. It is doubly difficult in this post-modern age. Dying to self leaves the rest of the body without needed members to keep the body functioning. The eye can't say to the ears, "I have no need of you," but it seems to be attempting this very thing in our narcissistic age.

When is the last time you have seen real leadership modeling dying to self? Where are the heroes when we need them? Why do we play to the selfish rather than the selfless? Sermons and classes could do a really good deed for kingdom service. Groups could discuss ways of moving to more selflessness and begin work groups that would allow the church to get into the community with deeds that reflect well on the Servant of all servants, Jesus Christ.

The often-heard comment in today's church is, "My needs are not being met." This, too, should be listened to carefully. When such a person complains that he is not being fed or his needs are not being met, he may be simply frustrated, or he may truly feel that sense of being neglected or isolated. Be careful, criticism often comes from anger more than from real differences. Other more serious problems may lurk under the guise of anger.

The listener who looks deeply in the eyes of a brother might find the problem is deeper than we realized. A brother's selfishness might be only symptomatic of a deeper malady. It might do us good to remember that work is produced by faith, labor is prompted by love and endurance is inspired by hope (1 Thessalonians 1:3).

Symptom Two: Negativism

Let me suggest that you get a group together and have a listening exercise. First let the group be free to list everything that is wrong with the church. You will have to do this in rapid succession and everyone is free to speak without censure.

Now turn around and let the same group make a list of what is right with the church. It will take a little prompting to get this list going, but don't give up too soon. Whatever way it turns out, the first list will be the longest in 90% of the churches. Why is this?

I would suggest that **we simply had rather talk about what is wrong than what is right**. Notice that when you are just sitting around chewing the fat, most of the conversation is negative. If you want to know how to settle the problems of the world, just join in a local coffee shop conversation. Perhaps it's our fallen human nature to be negative and some of us have a hard time overcoming it. We can act out of sheer cussedness, even while justifying our actions to ourselves.

Complaints often start with church leaders as objects. For some reason church leaders seem to be a lightning rod that draws the power of the storm. Even the Apostle Paul was not exempt. The churches in Galatia attacked his apostleship. They had convinced themselves that he was not an authentic apostle and that he had made the message more appealing to the Gentiles by removing from the gospel certain legal requirements. The disgruntled in Corinth challenged his personal integrity and his authority as an apostle. If this sounds all too familiar for our day, remember that human nature hasn't changed a lot and the Devil is still sowing seeds of disharmony in the body. For some there is no hammer for building but only for destroying.

Many of us get discouraged more with complainers than with anything else that we deal with. Complaining is as powerful as dynamite, as contagious as measles, and as corrosive as acid. Perhaps a new way of looking at critics is in order. Charles Spurgeon made a comment about those who find fault. "Get a friend to tell you your faults, or better still, welcome an enemy who will watch you keenly and sting you savagely. What a blessing such an irritating critic will be to the wise man, what an intolerable nuisance to a fool." The Proverbs say, "*He who listens to a life-giving rebuke will be at home among the wise*" (Proverbs 15:31). "*Better is open rebuke than hidden love*" (Proverbs 27:5). "*It is better to heed a wise man's rebuke than to listen to the song of fools*" (Ecclesiastes 7:5).

Negative discussion rarely leads to positive, practical action. After hearing about an hour's worth of negatives and how the critic didn't like the way the leader was doing things, the leader finally got in a word. He said a mouthful when he said, "How would you begin solving the problem?" It is easy to find fault. It is more difficult to find solutions. There seems to be an old refrain of a song that I heard lots of years ago that keeps coming to my mind. "Accentuate the positive, eliminate the negative and don't fool around with Mr. In-between." There is power in negative thinking and there is power in positive thinking. The power of one is destructive. The power of the other is constructive. Let the leader lead in the positive and deal with the negative in a loving manner. Too much focus on the negative will destroy the church.

The leader must also realize that hypochondria is habit forming. Transformation of lives is the power of the gospel. Salvation without transformation should never be tolerated in our churches. It's not just about saying the right formulas and getting the "fire insurance" in place. One of the things the modern church is under-emphasizing is the power of the story of Jesus to change lives. We need the Martha's of the church to come and sit at His feet and learn of Him.

Negativism is a terrible problem, but is it only symptomatic of a deeper problem? Are we fighting men of straw, or do we need to learn to joust with real villains?

Symptom Three: Communication Breakdown

Almost every church is heard to complain, "We have a **communication problem**." One of the things our elders are always looking at is how to improve communication. There are many situations where some person is in need of information and it does not arrive on time. We could use a little FedEx system of communication in our churches. Maybe the information would get there on time.

I often hear complaints by ministry leaders, teachers, and members that they don't know what is going on. For some reason the word gets bogged down somewhere, and the people remain in darkness. Some churches have begun family meetings where they share information with each other. Other churches have set aside time during the Sunday morning worship where family concerns may be shared.

Sometimes leaders seem to think that information about what is going on locally is best held in private. Or perhaps it just seems that way to the ordinary member. Most churches are lacking a vehicle for good communication. The bulletin can serve a good purpose, but much needed information never makes it to the pages of the local bulletin, or is seldom read by many members when it is there.

I see leaders getting together to discuss the communication problems; but because they never can agree on the causes and solutions, the conversation dries up. The result is that the church runs on autopilot and ministries operate on habit.

Perhaps communication is not the real problem in this case; working with the symptom will get us nowhere. Until the real problem is addressed, we probably will continue to flounder in this crucial area.

Symptom Four: Open Conflict

Have you ever noticed that when you really get serious about being the church that **open conflicts** seem to surface? Could it be that the Devil gets in the foray and adds fuel to the fire? One church had been dealing with open conflict that had stymied the work for more than a year. When someone asked what the problem was, the answer came as a multi-headed monster. Nobody could boil the conflict down into one thing. It was so diverse that most were not even sure how it started.

There are few counselors who are not familiar with this

scenario. A couple comes in the office and begins therapy. They begin to argue, and the counselor allows it to continue. Now for the big question, "What are we arguing about?" In 90% of the cases neither can tell the counselor what the argument is about. They pile so much garbage on the table that they don't have a chance of settling anything. The garbage only creates more hostility, and the Devil has his day.

We fight over everything from budget to youth, from times of worship to preachers. Little irritations and big ones come at us so fast that it becomes difficult to keep our footing. People get discouraged and leave this church. Sometimes they leave Jesus.

Conflict in the church is often the outward problem when we meet to decide the health of the body. The eyes seem to be clouded, and the light is not making its way to the church or the community around it. The Apostle Paul was told by Jesus that he would be sent to *"Open their eyes and turn them from darkness to light, and from the power of Satan to God, so that they may receive forgiveness of sins and a place among those who have been sanctified by faith in me"* (Acts 26:18). Conflict allows the god of this age to blind the minds of unbelievers, so that they cannot see the light of the gospel of the glory of Christ who is the image of God (2 Corinthians 4:4). If we are to let the light make everything visible, we will need to heed the admonition: *"Wake up, O sleeper, rise from the dead, and Christ will shine on you"* (Ephesians 5:14).

Conflict must be managed if the church is to move ahead. If a patient is bleeding, the first move is to stop the bleeding. If the church is conflicting, the first step is to stop the conflicting. But once the truce is agreed upon, the care giver must find the source of the bleeding, else the bleeding will begin again. What is the disease that is causing the problem? How can we get at it and help the body begin to mend?

Symptom five: Plateau or decline

Eighty-five percent of churches are in one of these stages. Churches have **plateaued** and may drift into decline if changes are not made in leadership and direction. Other churches have already begun the **decline**.

As I see it, there is a new awakening among churches. Doing business as usual is not getting the job done, and many leaders are looking for ways to move ahead. We are tired of below-level performance, and we are looking for ways to get off the plateau or reverse the decline. There are sure to be some churches that might throw out the baby with the bath water, but there are many more who will carefully study and evaluate and find ways to reverse trends and still be committed to Biblical principles. Preceding any change, there must be a clear recognition of those things which do not change.

Part of this reversal of directions must involve the move to the positive and eliminate the negative as a steady diet for the local church and its visitors. Modern seekers are not interested in what we are against, but they have a healthy interest in what we are for and what we are doing. The modern seeker is interested in being involved in a church that has an impact for good on the community and the world. Programs that help people get seriously involved in helping people in the community and making a difference globally will call for the best in people and will fire up the local body until people will come from all over to see the church burn for Christ.

These symptoms must be carefully evaluated and diagnosed. The sad fact is that these symptoms contribute to our problems in such dynamic ways that we have precious little time and energy left to correct the problems and grow. After the disease has been properly diagnosed, we will have to find the time and the energy to deal with the real problems and let the power of God shine in our local churches.

The Real Problem

Now to what I consider the real problem: "*Where there is no vision, the people perish*" (Proverbs 29:18, KJV). Lack of direction will leave the church in chaos. The eyes have told their tale and the diagnosis is that **there is no direction and vision** that can capture a church and let it see the possibilities that are clearly in focus. Much has been written about how to write clear mission statements, and I don't intend to get into that area. The reader can find any number of books and articles that will help write a clear mission statement. My concern is more specific to the idea of the mission that is embodied in the mission statement.

What I want to focus on here is the need for clear goals and definite plans to reach those goals. I remember well going fishing on one of the lakes in Tennessee. I had my little boat out on the lake and was doing my normal thing of not catching fish. Out on the lake it was a beautiful spring day and right after a lunch of Beanie Weenies, a nap seemed appropriate. There was no danger in the middle of the lake, so I dropped off to sleep in the bottom of the boat. I awoke suddenly and looked up. An ugly snake (aren't they all ugly?) was looking menacingly at me. I had drifted under a tree near the bank. Well, I got out of there as quickly as I could. Drifting is always dangerous, and I have refrained from it to this day. "That ancient serpent called the devil or Satan, who leads the whole world astray," is waiting for us to drift under his tree top.

When there is no vision for the local body, people follow their selfish desires. Self-interest prevails in a vacuum where no vision engages the mind. Stagnation easily follows, and discouragement sneaks in unheralded.

After completion of a building project, one goal is reached and another does not replace it. The church flounders and "*the harvest is past, the summer is ended and we are not saved*" (Jeremiah 8:20, KJV). Churches that are satisfied with maintenance rather than mission will find few people saved in the year's outreach.

When there is no vision, negativism takes the day. When there is no vision to be communicated, communication breaks down. When there is no vision, open conflict rules the relationships because there is no single cause that pulls people together. When the local leadership provides no vision, churches plateau and decline.

Without clear vision, growth will be stunted because "everybody does what is right in his own eyes." Existing programs plateau and new programs are nonexistent or they die in infancy. Self-interest goes against the very tenor of the teaching of Jesus: *"If anyone would come after me, he must deny himself and take up his cross and follow me"* (Matthew 16:24).

As an old goal is reached, another must take its place or the church will lose its direction. Achieved goals not replaced by new ones merely open the door for ailments to enter the body, and the eye will become darkness.

Keeping people working together means that they must be working toward something. "A horse can't kick while pulling and can't pull while kicking." Do the leaders share a vision? Do the ministry leaders share that vision? Do all staff members have an investment in the vision? Do old members have a clear understanding of the vision? Are new members immediately exposed to the vision? *"Where there is no vision, the people perish."*

Steps to Good Health

So, steps to good health may be found in a clear vision. We have looked into the eyes, and found the disease. We have stopped the bleeding; now it is time to move ahead for the Lord. These simple, yet complex, steps will lead us out of the hospital and back to work.

Step One: The church must have a purpose and a vision understood and supported by all its members.

Step Two: The leaders must develop a strategy for accomplishing this vision.

Step Three: Both staff and members clearly understand how their involvement contributes to the purpose and outreach of the church, and they are accountable for the accomplishment of their assignments.

Step Four: The healthy church knows how to party. It looks for small successes and actively celebrates them.

Step Five: It must be a shared vision if anything is going to be accomplished other than burnout.

One of our ladies' classes recently began a study of Nancy Eichman's book *Keeping Your Balance*. As I am writing this chapter I came across this book and found some jewels that seem appropriate here. On page 17 Nancy gives some sayings that might help us chew on this subject with a bit more meditation.

> "There is more to life than increasing speed." Mohandas Gandhi
>
> "It is an old and ironic habit of human beings to run faster when we have lost our way." Rollo May
>
> "Make haste slowly." Benjamin Franklin
>
> "It isn't so much how busy you are, but why you are busy. The bee is praised; the mosquito is swatted." Unknown
>
> "Don't run through life so fast that you forget not only where you've been, but also where you are." Brian Dyson
>
> "The world is moving so fast these days that the man who says it can't be done is generally interrupted by someone doing it." Elbert Hubbard

Have you heard the joke about NATO? No Action, Talk Only. This could be said about some churches; there is a lot of talk but little action. To be effective we must move beyond the talk stage.

We must also move beyond the planning stage. An old sales motto that I have heard for years says, "Plan your work and work your plan." Petronius Arbiter, an author in the court of Nero, once wrote: "We trained hard, but it seemed that every time we were beginning to form up into teams we would be reorganized. I was to learn late in life that we tend to meet any new situation by reorganizing; and a wonderful method it can be for creating the illusion of progress while producing confusion, inefficiency and demoralization."

Are we ever guilty of this method of operating? We sit and plan. We talk about the church, its purpose and mission. We get excited about it and then go back to doing business as usual. Perhaps we could use an infusion of the Nike commercial: "Just Do It!"[1]

Discussion Questions

1. What "symptom" is most meaningful to you? Be prepared to discuss it.

2. Can you add other steps for good health?

3. Which of the quotes in this chapter helped you the most?

4. How can the Nike slogan help you?

---

[1] Some of these thoughts were adapted from an article in Leadership Magazine, Summer, 1992, P 76 - by Donald Gerig and Gary Litwiller

Chapter 6
Two Continuums:
Tasks vs. Relationships and
Goals vs. People

You can have two kinds of leaders in a local church. There can also be combinations of these leadership styles. The first is the **goal-oriented leader** and the second is the **people-oriented leader.** Depending upon the makeup of the church and the needs of the moment, the choice of styles will have different outcomes.

Goal-Oriented Leaders

The goal-oriented leader is one who **takes complete control**. He will allow little input and will be totally in the driver's seat. He usually is a good short-term trouble shooter and will come in and make the difficult decisions to get the crisis behind them and get the church poised for moving ahead. I will first discuss the areas where each functions better; then I will discuss the behaviors that accompany each of these orientations.

Goal-oriented leaders function best when there is **confusion and chaos.** That's why this leadership style is sometimes called "Trouble Shooting." When a church is in confusion, there is little progress that can be made. Any leaders who try to lead will be able only to manage crisis and put out fires. Most leaders will not even be able to accomplish this much.

There is another more diabolical thing that occurs in some churches when confusion and chaos prevail. Churches can chew up and spit out leaders as a bass rises to the top of the water and attempts to spit out the lure. *"If you keep on biting and devouring each other, watch out or you will be destroyed by each other"* (Galatians 5:15). We went into a church like that in a major town in the north-central states. When we arrived to try to put out some fires and save the church from self-destruction, members had already chewed up and spit out any leader who had any gifts in this area. After talking to several of these leaders who had been summarily dispatched to an early leaders' grave, we knew that the things they needed were the gifts of a trouble shooter. Now good trouble shooters are hard to find and even harder to keep, but I am convinced that there are some who are gifted in this area. After a trouble shooter leader arrived on the scene, things were manageable, and confusion was reduced. Then the church was ready to dispatch the trouble shooter for another leader of a differing style. One of the things you have to watch out for is that some trouble shooters want to stay too long, and the confusion and chaos will return because now the church needs a person of a different leadership style.

Another time when goal-oriented leaders function well is when there are **lots of dependent personalities**. A newly planted church is an example of this type. Also, there will be times when the local church is composed of persons who have not grown and developed their social and spiritual skills to the point that they can make quality efforts without strong goal-oriented leaders. Some entrepreneurial types have formed businesses that continue to be run by goal-oriented leaders. Such a business is heavy on authoritarian concepts and is run by the power that the leader has by virtue of his ownership of the business.

There are few churches that can be run like a one-man business; and those that try often find themselves disgruntled, disillusioned, and disembarked.

Inertia is the tendency for an object in motion to remain in motion or for an object at rest to remain at rest. This latter condition is apparent in all too many churches. Jesus wrote a letter to the messenger of the church in Ephesus warning that they could cease to exist as a church as their candlestick was removed. The warning was the result of their leaving their first love. *"Remember the height from which you have fallen! Repent and do the things you did at first"* (Revelation 2: 5).

When a church is in the state of inertia, the task-oriented leadership style can help get it off dead center and moving ahead. It requires lots of power to get it going. As with an automobile, the most power is used in moving from a dead start to a moving object. Only the leaders with definite plans and the power to start the engines will be able to do anything for this church. But there are certain gifted individuals who can come in and get things rolling with goals and plans to meet those goals.

Goal-oriented leaders work best when **a short-term result** is sought. Anytime a leader must take complete control, you will find only short-term goals to be possible. Dictators often come to the front during chaotic times and look to be a good solution for the problems that are tearing a church or a country down. A dictator works well for the short term, but a church will not want to remain in this mode for long. The leaders with gifts will quickly clash and, if they lose, go other places where their gifts can be used better.

If you have received the impression that I am not in favor of strong goal-oriented leaders, you are not entirely correct. I see the need for this leadership style in some churches during tough times. There is biblical authority for leaders who ask their sheep to follow and *"Obey your leaders and submit to their authority"* (Hebrews 13:17).

Some would argue that this command is in the middle voice that requires us to view this leadership as "participation with your leaders" and does not demand absolute obedience. To this I agree. Jesus is the only absolute authority for his church.

People-Oriented Leaders

Using the business model of leadership, the opposite of goal-oriented leaders would be people-oriented leaders. You might have noticed that I always look for balance because I feel very strongly that this is the only way to growth. I would certify to all that, while I discuss the characteristics of each style, I am really arguing for balance.

As we look at the opposite of goal-oriented leadership, be assured that I am not looking to this exclusively, but in today's culture all churches had better have a good percentage of people-oriented leaders. I know that people-oriented leaders work best when **relational issues are important**. In our culture of the 21st century, relational issues have taken a big leap toward a place of first importance. One might argue that relationships will outweigh doctrinal issues in most churches today. When push comes to shove, most modern-day people will opt for relationships over doctrine.

I might also argue that the greatest doctrine taught in Scripture is **love**. *"Now these three remain: faith, hope and love. But the greatest of these is love"* (1 Corinthians 13:13). We don't want to miss the greatest in our hunt for "doctrinal" purity.

In churches that have gone through a storm, it is necessary to have leadership that can major in **mending relationships**. Leaders who can hear, really hear, what people are saying and sense what they are feeling are hard to find, but they can be developed. The church could use a good dose of leaders who can encourage the full expression of feelings and not become reactionaries. People-oriented leaders can lead where most are afraid to travel. Leaders would do well to spend a bit of time with Stephen Covey's first habit of highly effective people: Be proactive.

People-oriented leaders are important **where emotions are high**. Most of us have been in an environment that is almost like an electrical storm, and lightning flashes, followed by thunder, are making noise that drowns out sanity. At any moment it seems possible that the group will implode.

It is during times like these that leaders are tested to the brink. When emotions are running rampant, it's almost like a runaway train. Getting out of its way seems to be the only choice for us. But good people-oriented leaders know that emotions are not evil or righteous; they are just there.

Smart leaders think of emotions and reason like two oars on a rowboat. One oar is emotion. The other oar is reason. As long as there is a semblance of balance between the two, the boat will go in the general directions we want to go. But let either get too powerful, and the boat begins to go in a circle. You can think of an emotion-laden church as a boat with Arnold Schwarzenegger on the emotional oar and Don Knotts on the reason oar.

What happens in lots of churches is that the powerful emotions take over, and Arnold's muscles lead the boat to circle more and more rapidly. It's not long before the swirl produces a deadly sinkhole that drowns the whole group.

Good people-oriented leaders can defang this deadly serpent and allow emotions their proper place without letting them defeat the church by self-destruction. *"If you keep on biting and devouring each other, watch out or you will be destroyed by each other"* (Galatians 5:15).

This brings us to the next asset of people-oriented leaders. While the battles are being fought, and after the battle is done, **we need healing**. Somewhere in the reading of Dietrich Bonhoffer I recall the statement: "The important thing is that there be no more wounds."

Leaders can't expect the patient to be fully healed in a few days after a major surgery. That kind of thing happens in Science-fiction movies and sitcoms on television, not in churches. People need time to heal from the wounds of battle. Most of us have been in churches where power has "solved" a problem, but the bleeding continues. Even in churches where problems have been met and most have moved on, there are many who haven't come to forgiveness and still need the kindness of leaders who carefully manage feelings and provide care for the walking wounded. Where healing is needed, we will need people-oriented leaders to stand by their flock and feed and nurture them as needed.

Finally, there is one other area where people-oriented leaders function better. In all churches there are times of **strain on relationships**. Where these strains occur, there is no substitute for time. When time is required, people-oriented leaders do a good job. They stay with their sheep who have struggled to keep the faith in the midst of difficult circumstances, and these sheep will need leaders who give them room to forgive and move on. Many will need years and spiritual maturing before they can re-enter the battle with the vim and vigor that are required of those who finish the race.

Discovering Your Leadership Style

So what kind of leader are you? You will probably lean to one or the other style. If you are more task-oriented, you will see people in relation to a mission or goal. The people-oriented leader will work on fairness, being easily approachable and have an instinct for giving comfort.

The best way to recognize your dominant style is to look at the ways you react in given situations. The task-oriented person will tend to restore structure and react to things not getting done. The people-oriented leader will more than likely respond to feelings of others and try to ease anxiety for the moment. "One fears that someone will be offended. The other fears that something won't get done." (David Luecke and Samuel Southard, *Pastoral Administration*, p. 19. See also their discussion of this subject in the first chapter of their book. The following material is adapted from this book.)

The behaviors that follow each of these orientations will be apparent and will help us identify what is happening and determine the best way to go. The following discussion of behaviors that conform to the different orientations will help you become a better leader. It will help if you will compare the two orientations and have a more lengthy discussion with other leaders in your quest for balance. It can prove helpful to identify where each leader is and how best to balance the whole group by using the best of all to accomplish the most.

The idea is that if we have two leaders who are people-oriented and two who are goal-oriented, we can develop a good balance in the leadership of a church. The more leaders we have the better chance of achieving a balance that can be conducive to solid growth for the future and accomplishing the purpose for which we have been called.

People-Oriented Leaders

People-oriented leaders are prone to put suggestions of others to work. Their listening antennae are up and functioning. They will take the suggestions of others and get to them immediately. Because they treasure people, they will want to help others achieve their goals and will work hard to help them reach them. This type of leader will honor people and will often be asking, "What suggestions do you have?"

In a church with these leaders, you will find a bottom-up approach to church programs. Members will feel they are heard and their suggestions are acted upon. You will usually find a satisfaction within the congregation and a friendship among members.

People-oriented leaders are also looking out for the welfare of individual members. With good people orientation there will be fewer people who fall through the cracks and are absent for months before leaders are aware they have been missing. With a good group of people-oriented leaders, there is less likelihood that the welfare of members is left to chance. These leaders will naturally look to the members for direction, and the welfare of members will be the driving force for the church.

These leaders are friendly and approachable. Their meetings are open, and members are encouraged to attend. Even the tenor of the meetings is more pastoral than administrative. Most members feel they can go to the leaders with whatever problems they have and will get a fair hearing. They will feel that there is real care for members of the body. *"Its parts should have equal concern for each other"* (1 Corinthians 12:25).

These leaders will discourage criticism and censoring of group behavior. Because they are oriented toward the people, they will be less likely to impugn the motives of others. They will listen carefully and lovingly to all sides and make an evaluation that is in keeping with their love for people.

You will not find these leaders engaging in harsh criticism or allowing the same to be voiced in the church. Where these leaders are dominant, there will be peace and harmony. The problem is that there is also peace and harmony in the cemetery. Where a church has only people-oriented leaders, you have difficulty moving ahead because you don't have the balance that is needed for reaching goals. This is one of those places you might want to stop and compare a goal-oriented behavior for balance.

People-oriented leaders will engage in little things that will make being a part of this local church pleasant. When leaders pay attention to members, you will find that the majority will feel good about their membership in that church. There will be a pleasant atmosphere in the church that allows others to feel loved and be given the opportunity to love in return.

It is a good feeling to be a part of a church where care is apparent and encouraged. When visitors come, they can feel that special something that makes them want to return. Some leaders are just about doing good and are often seen living where others live and making the environment pleasing to others. This church attracts people and will help more people than they can comfortably address.

Leaders who are people-oriented are on a first-name basis with each other. Formal titles and designations are not used among these leaders. Titles separate people, and people-oriented leaders shun the use of anything that may detach them from others in the church. Friendliness and personal relationships are more important than distinctions.

People-oriented leaders will always think of the opinions of others before they go ahead with a program or project. They will always take the temperature of the local church before designing activities that might be important to others. Because they are people-oriented, they will want to consult as many as possible before going ahead. Opinions of others are greatly valued.

Meetings are different for people-oriented leaders. The atmosphere is friendly and often jokes are shared and friendships are enhanced during meetings. This can drive those goal-oriented leaders to tears. The latter want to get on with the meeting and the former want to get on with their relationships. A balance in leaders will make for a good meeting.

The last characteristic of people-oriented leaders is that they are slow in taking sides in cases of disagreement. You could guess that this is true because they are other-focused. Disagreements are smoothed over for the sake of people. Danger lurks in the woodwork if this is the only way conflict is handled. This is another case for balance in the leadership of local churches.

Goal-Oriented Leaders

Let's consider again **Goal-oriented leaders**. What are the characteristics of people who are goal-oriented? They are certainly people who pay close attention to tasks and getting the job done. In fact, to them, the task is more important than people.

If you are a goal-oriented person, your behavior will exhibit the following tendencies.

You will plan the day's activities in detail. You will be interested in details and more details. The success you will feel at day's end will be based on how much of the day you could anticipate and how well you accomplished your goals for that day. Palm Pilots and day timers and appointment calendars are the tools of your trade. You go into a meeting with a well-planned agenda in hand. CEOs are leaders who know when, where, and why things are happening. They don't like to be caught off guard in a meeting or in an activity. They will most likely be the ones who write out everything they want to see happen and have a carefully thought-out time schedule that will be followed.

Goal-oriented leaders will attempt to maintain definite standards of performance. Poor performance can so frustrate goal-oriented leaders that they can leave the group, job, or even community. Many churches lose good leaders through frustration. These leaders' expectations can be pushed aside by people-oriented leaders, and tasks never quite get finished. Good leaders on both sides can leave in frustration.

These goal-oriented leaders are good at letting members know what is expected of them. These leaders are not afraid to ask much of the members, and they strongly expect things to happen. We have learned through research and observation that members of the body work better and stay longer when there are clear expectations and they are challenged by what they can do for others in the body. Growing churches have learned to close the back door by keeping new members involved in meaningful activities. That is why goal-oriented leaders must be allowed to balance those leaders who are people-oriented. (See Thom Ranier's book *Surprising Insights From the Unchurched and Proven Ways to Reach Them*, Chapter five).

Not only do these leaders let members know what is expected of them, but they are first in getting things done. They don't just hand out assignments and wait for a task to be accomplished. They are on the front line and in the trenches where the action is. They lead by example. They don't urge others to go and do what they refuse to go and do. You don't find these leaders urging personal evangelism and not doing it. They are the first to be there and be on the job. God's church needs these leaders who are there leading in clear sight of the flock.

Another characteristic of goal-oriented leaders is that they emphasize the meeting of deadlines. While the people-oriented leaders are nurturing and listening and empathizing, the goal-oriented leaders are looking for accountability. It becomes a difficult thing to build accountability into the work of the local church, but where you have none you lose the real game of spiritual growth. Shoddy work and lame excuses never built strong churches or strong people. These leaders will push themselves and others to set and meet deadlines.

In order for this to happen, goal-oriented leaders will keep the work moving at a rapid pace. We put a project together several years ago and asked a member who was a national sales manager for a large multinational industry to supervise the project. He worked us through the plans and led with enthusiasm. He let us know what was expected and continually emphasized the meeting of deadlines. He was there to insure that we kept moving at a rapid pace. The goals were accomplished, and all who participated were joyful.

One of the things we learned from this dynamic leader was that we needed carefully thought-out organizational lines. He was not fearful of asking us to follow organizational lines. This increased communication at all levels and insured that information flowed in the right direction and to the right people. This also allowed us to see that the work of all members was coordinated.

Another thing we learned from this dynamic salesperson was that you can be critical of poor work and not offend people. He was able to get the most from all of us without making us feel that we had failed. Being critical of poor work is not an easy task, and that is why most of us avoid it like the plague. It can be done in a loving manner, but it will need some help from the people-oriented leaders.

One of the final things that we learned from this project was that he saw to it that our staff members were working to capacity. That was one of the toughest assignments of all.

Now you may be thinking that I am saying that one orientation is better than the other, but I would hasten to assure you that I believe we need both of these orientations in a church that seeks to be balanced. No individual leader will be completely in one corner or the other. Each can work for balance but will certainly lean toward either people or goals. I do not see this as an "either/or" but a "both/and" situation. A group of leaders can serve as a balancing act as they understand who they are and how they can work together for God. God has gifted individuals in different ways. We must allow leaders to lead in their gifted areas, and as leaders we must seek the gifts of all so that the body can grow and build *"itself up in love, as each part does its work"* (Ephesians 4:16).

Discussion Questions

1. When is "goal oriented" leadership appropriate?

2. When is "people oriented" leadership appropriate?

3. Which style of leadership is your natural tendency?

4. Can you think of a time when your natural style was less-than-effective?

Chapter 7
What Kind of Leader Will You Follow?

Think of the persons that you would follow in almost any situation. What are the qualities they will need to possess? What kind of leaders have you respected in your own history and what made you follow these leaders with confidence? You might want to sit down and list two or three leaders you have followed in your past and write a list of qualities that each person had that gave you the motivation and the confidence to follow.

In this chapter I will develop some general leadership qualities that will help us develop as leaders and as followers. Followership might give us a bit of help in the qualities that are most desirous in our church leaders. It might be helpful for the reader to look at the life of Jesus and think of incidents where the Master exhibited some of these attributes.

Compassion

The first quality that I look for in a person that I will follow is **compassion**. In times of chaos we might want a trouble shooter who will force peace by raw power. This person comes on the scene with guns smoking and heads fall. Although there might be a need for a "benevolent dictator" at times, under most circumstances, these are only temporary solutions and churches will not serve long under a dictator.

"Therefore, as God's chosen people, holy and dearly loved, clothe yourself with compassion, kindness, humility, gentleness and patience" (Colossians 3:12).

"And the Lord's servant must not quarrel; instead he must be kind to everyone, able to teach, not resentful" (2 Timothy 2:24).

Why is it that we don't care how much another knows until we know that he cares? For some reason humans have been programmed to quickly zoom in on compassion. It's like honey attracting flies. Even a small child can usually tell if a person cares about them or cares only for himself. Because leaders watch for our souls (Hebrews 13:17) we want them to be filled with compassion for us and our families and for the Lord Jesus.

We can be fooled for a while. Haven't we all? But in the long run real compassion will come to the top and we will only follow the persons who demonstrate love on a daily bases, over the long haul. As I was being driven to the airport to fly to Maui (I'm writing this in Maui), one of our members told the story about being in Oklahoma and helping a family with some gas money. He told them if they came through Dickson, Tennessee to stop if they needed gas money. A short time later this family showed up on Sunday morning in need of fuel to get them to their journey's end. Walter spotted them and was standing and talking with them after worship. One of our elders walked up and met them and found out their dilemma. He immediately pulled out a $20 bill and gave it to them. Walter continues to serve under this leader who is full of compassion.

Compassion is one of those characteristics that you can fake a while but not for long. The true character comes to the front and will sour everything it touches. Followers will flock to those who demonstrate compassion and will linger far behind those who lack it.

Since the scriptures clearly say to "clothe yourself with compassion," that would mean that compassion is attainable for all leaders. It is within every man's challenge to *"turn from evil and do good; seek peace and pursue it"* (Psalms 34:14). John records the words of Jesus in John 13:34-35: *"A new command I give to you: Love one another. As I have loved you, so you must love one another. By this shall all men know that you are my disciples if you have love for one another."* Jesus would not have commanded something that was out of our reach as leaders.

Notice three things about these verses.

First, it is a command. Not a suggestion or a wish list. It is as strong as Jesus could make it. Do it or be disobedient.

Second, it is a distinct command. *"By this all men will know that you are my disciples."* The real mark of Jesus' people is still love.

Third, it is a distinctly difficult command. Jesus never said it would be easy. He just said do it like he did it.

Leaders that compel followers will be full of compassion. Harmony can be attained in the local church when leaders are *"sympathetic, love as brothers"* and *"compassionate and humble"* (1 Peter 3:8). Spending time in the biggest room in anybody's house—the room for improvement—can pay great dividends in the Lord's church.

There is one other point that I would like to make before leaving this area. God never said to try to do better. He says that we are to train ourselves to be godly (1 Timothy 4:7). Training is one of the ways we become better leaders and better lovers. Will we get in the gym and start training to be God's leaders, full of compassion?

Preparation

The concept of training naturally leads to the next characteristic of leaders, **preparation**.

How do people prepare to be leaders? What adequate preparations are there that might enhance the leaders in the local church?

I recently attended a workshop for church leaders on conflict management. It was conducted by two experts in the field and the presentations were very helpful. Less that 10% of the leaders in the area had made any attempt to attend. It would have been a time for preparation and learning. Training leaders is sometimes like pulling teeth.

Yet, most leaders I talk to or work with have a keen feeling that they are not adequately prepared to do the leading necessary to keep the church as a leading tool for outreach and encouragement. In conversation leaders are wanting more help in the shepherding of souls and the watching over the flock. In practice it looks to be far from happening. Books like this one are in every bookstore and are even in some of our libraries. Some of our better leaders are actually reading them to the profit of the churches they lead.

However, when we think realistically, most people learn their leadership skills, or lack thereof, on the job. If we look at the biblical model of training leaders, we are impressed with the fact that most leaders were trained on the job. They learned leadership by following a leader and letting that leader show them the ropes. Timothy learned by doing under the careful eye of Paul. Even Paul might have learned some valuable leadership qualities under the tutelage of Barnabas.

One of the churches where I worked conducted a Camp for Future Leaders. It was for high school young people who want to look to the future and be prepared. For a week these young people were exposed to models of leaders from the area. They studied scriptures and read books on leadership. They are not today's leaders, but they will be leaders in the future. They will now go back to their youth groups and put into practice the things learned. For the next several years they will be trained on the job for dynamic leadership in local churches.

There is another program called "Lads to Leaders" that has become a training ground for future leaders. More intentional work is going to have to be done if the quality of leaders in the church is to increase.

Marshal Keeble, a preacher of a generation past, always carried young men with him when he went to preach. He would have them read scriptures and sometimes make short talks. Daily he would talk with them and ask them questions. From this pool of young men came some of the great preachers in the African American churches of the present.

Is it only in the church that we select leaders who are just there and expect miracles of them? Maybe we could make some definite plans to have leaders undergo careful preparation as they move into this important role in the church.

One of the things I found most helpful in my work at Fuller Seminary was the insistence on studying models of successful churches. The churches around Pasadena, California, are probably the most studied churches in the world. Some of the most valuable preparation might be to go and spend some time with leaders that have shown they are making good progress in the care and keeping of souls. On-the-job training can enhance our leadership skills and make the church a better place for worship and working.

Faithfulness

One of the characteristics that leaders must have if they are to have a steady following is **faithfulness**. Faithfulness is loyalty in work and life. Personal integrity: don't leave home without it.

"Now it is required that those who have been given a trust must prove faithful" (1 Corinthians 4:2). It hasn't been long since most of us have been exposed to the people who speak out of both sides of their mouths. This was even a problem in Jesus' day: *"But do not do what they do, for they do not practice what they preach"* (Matthew 23:3).

People who must please all men must get into politics and learn to play the game well. Not so with God's leaders. *"Simply let your 'Yes' be 'Yes' and your 'No' be 'No'; anything beyond this comes from the evil one"* (Matthew 5:37). As I write this I am reminded of the leader who was accused of saying one thing when he was with one group and another when he was with another group. My brothers these things ought not to be! Caught in the political arena, leaders can lose the confidence of the country and be forced to resign under pressure as made famous in the often told Watergate days.

Speaking truth in love is not only the better policy but the only policy open to God's leaders. Some may be thinking that I am wasting some good space by preaching to the choir, but let Paul remind us that each one *"must put off falsehood and speak truthfully to his neighbor, for we are all members of one body"* (Ephesians 4:25).

In the body we must demand openness and free communication. Leaders are accountable to the local followers to communicate truth openly and freely. A church in an unnamed state was running into all kinds of leadership problems. After a thorough investigation, it was clear that the leaders had not openly communicated to those who were expected to foot the bill about what was going on. All confidence was lost in these leaders and the church was in chaos. One of the problem areas that we often found in trying to mediate disputes in churches was the lack of full and fair communication between leaders and followers. When will we learn to trust Jesus' words and our brothers' intelligence?

We will follow leaders who are open and honest. We will most often trust their leadership and support their programs. But we will not follow the leader who says and does not do. Where integrity is concerned, we will look for leaders who are faithful to the trust given them.

At this point I will hit a topic that has received lots of attention in the last few years. It is not my intent to give additional or old material that others have already written volumes on. But it still needs to be said that people will follow leaders who exhibit Servanthood. *"Whoever wants to become great among you must be your servant, and whoever wants to be first must be your slave"* (Matthew 20:26-27). *"For whoever exalts himself will be humbled, and whoever humbles himself will be exalted"* (Matthew 23:12). *"Though I am free and belong to no man, I make myself a slave to everyone, to win as many as possible"* (1 Corinthians 9:19).

Service

Leaders who train themselves to have the mind of Christ will learn to take the position of a **servant** as did the Master (Philippians 2:5-11). These are the leaders who will get a healthy following in our age and will be the kinds of leaders who can see healthy bodies develop and grow. God needs leaders who are not hirelings who will run when the heat is on. He needs leaders who can stand the heat in the kitchen and serve the meal with humility and love. The mind of a servant will move a leader to stay in the kitchen, even when the heat is on. As others fade at the moment of difficulty, the servant-leader will stick like Elmer's Glue. Servants are long-haulers and followers will know that in times of strain, they will not be forsaken.

Problem Solvers

Leaders must develop **problem-solving skills** that stay them through difficult times. I am appalled that so few leaders have any training in managing differences. We mostly learn what we have learned by observing and trial and error. We solve problems in our homes the way our parents did or the exact opposite way. I have even noticed that managers in corporations have learned good skills at work but seem to forget these when they come home or attend church.

There are a few of our universities that are now offering degrees in dispute resolution. Many para-church organizations are now offering leadership training with a module on problem-solving. The sad thing is that this often does not trickle down to the local church. I am a firm believer in intentionality. Leaders must intentionally train to be leaders and part of this training will be a healthy dose of Getting to Yes. (See Roger Fisher and others who have written much on this subject.)

Why not get your leaders together and spend a quarter studying and working through a good book on the subject.

This would serve two purposes. You can learn skills that will help build a healthy approach to inevitable conflict and you will get to know the personalities and skills of each member of the group.

Empathetic

We want leaders who can **feel** the same things we feel. We want leaders to **understand** the struggles we are going through. We want them to listen all the way through our pain and not jump to quick and ineffective ways of dealing with the headache with simplistic answers that sound like "Take two aspirin and call me in the morning." There are times we don't need a sermon or a quick fix. We just need our leaders to exhibit the empathy that will help us trust the leader and eventually allow this leader to lead and guide us into a more abundant life.

A few years ago a church that I was consulting with was in total chaos. One of the members remarked that the current leaders did not have any feelings: "They just don't feel." Now I understand that this is an exaggeration, but when leaders really develop empathy, there will develop a different scenario in the local church.

Some might argue that I am confusing sympathy with empathy and that could be the case. What I want us to understand is that as we are saved by the grace of God and we should always remember that *"God opposes the proud, but gives grace to the humble"* (James 4:6). So all of us should *"humble yourselves before the Lord, and he will lift you up"* (James 4:10). Leaders can be *"kind and compassionate to one another, forgiving each other, just as in Christ God forgave you"* (Ephesians 4:32). Remembering from whence we have come will help the leaders to empathize with the brother of differing background and problems and pain.

I am willing to follow a leader who is willing to get down in the mud and work with me. I want to follow a leader who can convince me that he listens long to understand where I'm coming from and what my values and desires are. In each local church there are people at all levels of growth and maturity. Leaders must respect this diversity.

Non-Judgmental Listening

Leaders must learn to **listen non-judgmentally**. When a follower comes into the group, there must be full acceptance of the person where he or she is at the moment. Acceptance of the many diversities in appearances, values, growth, cultures, likes, dislikes, and perceptions are looked at non-judgmentally. Followers are like children; they will test the adult to see if they are fully accepted before they are willing to go along with that adult.

I am convinced that most people who visit our churches each week are there to test the waters. Sure, they come to look at the youth program, the nursery, and the facilities. They look at the worship and preaching. They look at their own perceived and real needs to see if this church will be able to meet them. They might even look at the Bible school classes to see if they will be uplifting for them. But the first and last thing they are looking for is acceptance. If they don't find this acceptance in the people, it's not there in the leaders, because leaders still set the tone for the personality of the local church.

As I was visiting with one of our members when I was in Maui, he was preparing a meal for workers in the homeless shelter. There were eleven workers that he had gotten to know as he had worked at the shelter for several months. How accepting do you think he is for people of diverse background and experience? Would leaders who spent a few days working with the homeless decrease or increase their acceptance of the people we are committed to reach? Going out into the "highways and byways" of our towns might increase our ability to be nonjudgmental.

When a new person arrives at your door, what is your attitude? Are we looking for people who are just like us in as many aspects as possible? Are we waiting for those who are on the same intellectual, financial, and growth level as we are before we welcome them? Are people who have had difficulty with finances, marriage, drugs and alcohol made to feel loved in our churches? Are leaders leading the way in feeding the hungry, giving a drink of water to the thirsty, welcoming the stranger, clothing the naked, and visiting the imprisoned? *"I tell you the truth, whatever you did for one of the least of these brothers of mine, you did for me"* (Matthew 25:40).

I sound like I'm preaching and I probably am. However, I'm not sure that we can lead where we have not gone. Until we have gone through the agony of wrestling with our own sins, we probably can't help others make progress in their journey. Until we have been with the saints in the mud and grime that is unsaintly, we probably will remain appraising people who turn many out of the kingdom and shut the doors to those who would enter.

Prayer

When prayer moves the arm that moves the world, leaders will be people with a **deep prayer life**. One of the leaders that I would have followed to almost any place was Jack Rollings. He was the most praying leader that I ever knew. It didn't matter much where he was he would pray. One day I met him in the aisle of a grocery store. As I was about to move on he started to praying. There we were in the aisle of the store beseeching God to bless our ministry. Now if he prayed for me in such unlikely places, I can be assured that he is praying for me in his daily prayers.

"Since the day we heard about you, we have not stopped praying for you and asking God to fill you with the knowledge of his will through all spiritual wisdom and understanding." It is this kind of prayer partner who helps the leader to lead and helps the follower to trust this leadership. Leaders who are much in prayer that we might *"live a life worthy of the Lord and may please him in every way: bearing fruit in every good work, growing in the knowledge of God and being strengthened with all power according to his glorious might so that*

you may have great endurance and patience" will be leaders that make it easy for us to follow (Colossians 1:9-11).

I have my doubts about the power of the leadership of the Jewish leaders who *"love to pray standing in the synagogues and on the street corners"* who *"keep on babbling like pagans"* (Matthew 6:5, 7). I can't see people lining up to follow such leaders. Long, impersonal, traditional and meaningless babble can't get you to the throne and can't inspire followers to get in step with the leader.

In a recent service, a lady came forward requesting prayers. I asked her what kind of prayer. Her answer was that she needed strength. I asked her what for. She looked at me and started to cry. Her son had gotten into the wrong crowd and was really rebellious. Her heart was broken and she didn't know where to turn but to her family in the local church. Suppose that I had left it as a simple prayer request, babbled a few words that seemed sincere, and gone on about the day? How would she have felt and what of others who needed to be praying specific and personal prayers for this lady? For the next week we all agreed to be prayer partners for her and made daily contact with her and some even prayed with her on the phone. Leadership is in need of a deep prayer life and getting personal about what we pray for and how we pray can move us in that direction.

We could offer the prayer of the disciples: *"Lord, teach us to pray"* (Luke 11:1). There are many good books on prayer that can be read with great profit. But the best place to learn is to go to the feet of Jesus and enter the closet with him. As we make prayer personal, we will find that others will follow our example and follow our lead in other areas as well.

Motivate

A praying leadership will provide the motivational style that is most likely to last for several generations. Leaders must **motivate** but not with the same tools that the world uses. *"The weapons we fight with are not the weapons of this world. On the contrary, they have divine power to demolish strongholds"* (2 Corinthians 10:4). Leaders are always looking for ways to motivate local churches to get on board with programs that have been conceived in their minds and they want the church to support these decisions. My own thoughts are that we need to get the people in on the conceiving of the plans and there won't be such a need to get them on board. Since they have been in on the planning, they will be in on the carrying out.

We are always looking for the right motivational leader who can do great superman feats. These types of leaders are few and far between. God has given all of us the power to lead by example. There is no greater motivation than to see that our leaders are leading in spiritual things. Only when the example is clear will we follow the leader.

Enthusiasm

The last kind of leader that I would follow is the **enthusiastic** leader. An enthusiastic leader will be both an example and a motivator. Enthusiasm is as powerful as dynamite and as contagious as the measles. From the beginning to the end of worship there must be an enthusiasm that is felt by all present.

Whatever we can do we must do it heartily. Enthusiasm can move mountains and move people. Local churches need local leaders who are joyful and expectant. Their enthusiasm must come from deep within, from a heart that is full of God. Enthusiasm means that God is inside and with God inside we will do whatever our hands find to do with a zest for the gospel that will inspire a church to build for God and reach the lost.

Most churches have wrestled with enthusiasm when making announcements. It is difficult to read a lot of announcements in an assembly without losing most of the audience. We have moved them to the end, or read them at the beginning, or flashed them on the screen, or handed out printed copies to try to make this communication effective. Nothing has been much of an improvement. I really like the way a church in Texas did their announcements. They would flash the announcement on the screen, followed by a picture of the person or family. It was done with care, and I could look at the pictures and pray for people whose faces I saw on the screen. It was done with care and enthusiasm.

Now go back to the list that you made at the beginning of this chapter. What qualities are missing from this chapter? Your list is a good or better than mine. What makes you follow a leader?

Discussion Questions

1. What is the biggest room in your house?

2. How would you describe a good leader?

3. Contrast your description with what James has in this chapter. What differences do you find?

4. How can we be more compassionate?

Chapter 8
Choosing a Model for Leadership

> **WANTED:** A new generation of Christian leaders for the 21st century. Must be willing to embody Christ and empower others. All interested parties are urged to apply.

It could be an ad in any religious paper.

As our world has moved into the new millennium, we need to take a penetrating and realistic look at Christian leadership from the perspective of Scripture and the example of Christ. It is a necessity to turn to any and every source to learn as much about leadership as we can. It would be healthful if we spent some time looking at leadership from the standpoint of what is taught in Scripture and what the life and times of Jesus can show.

"Leadership is one of the most observed and least understood phenomenon on the earth" (James McGregor Burns). Surveys taken asking "What is the greatest need in training leaders in the church?" have consistently found that more training for leaders in administration and people management is a high priority. "It is clearly understood that the rise and fall of membership depends far more on the strength and enthusiasm of leadership than on any theological viewpoint" (James Burns).

Finding Our Leadership Styles

But how do we determine our leadership style? How closely related is style to our psychological, cultural and sociological background? Are our own theological backgrounds a determining factor in what style of leadership we exhibit? Do temperament and personality play a vital part in how we lead?

My answer to these questions is a resounding "**Yes!**" Styles of leadership are affected by all of these issues. Psychologically we become an extension of our basic personality. Birth order and birth origin and genetic systems certainly play a vital part in the way we view things and thus our leadership style.

Sociologically, we are part of a child development system that started in the womb of our mother. Childhood experiences are a factor influencing who we are and how we think. What you learned in your family of origin certainly blesses or curses your present style of leadership. The teachers you had in school, your participation in activities, and even the friends you choose supply the ingredients of whom you are and what kind of leader you have become.

Culturally, if you come from a German background or if you are a "60s" child your style of leadership will be influenced. If you grew up in the south or the north or the west or the east or the Midwest, or even on a different continent, these factors will color the way you look at leadership. Even the job you do and the person you married will have importance in your view of leadership.

Theologically, you are a product of your history and thinking. Your understanding of submission and authority, the concept of chain of command, the feelings of control and obedience are all influenced by our understanding of God. These also have a way of affecting our view of Scripture and the teaching of the Bible on leadership.

I mention these to let you think through them with a clear mind. To neglect this is to go on with perceptions that can harm the local church. When leaders think that their style of leadership is directly from God and untainted by all these influences, it is highly unlikely that they will be able to meet the challenges that face us in the post-modern generation.

The Leader's Charge

Take a few moments and think about which is correct.
- A) A leader takes charge.
- B) A leader is given a charge.

Often we look for a leader who has the personality that can take off and run with the ball. This leader will have a proven track record in business and industry and has demonstrated that leadership comes easily from all perspectives.

Ask yourself the penetrating question "What leader do I know who has caused the most harm in the local church?" This leader will come under the category of the most unloving and unspiritual leader we have encountered. Church leadership has been full of self-seekers from the first to the present day. *"I wrote to the church, but Diotrephes, who loves to be first, will have nothing to do with us. So if I come, I will call attention to what he is doing, gossiping maliciously about us. Not satisfied with that, he refuses to welcome the brothers. He also stops those who want to do so and puts them out of the church"* (3 John 9, 10). Churches have become virtual tombs where no new people can get in and the old seem to be dying. New people are the life blood of a local church but where there are leaders who get stuck on power and authority for themselves, the church will stagnate and die.

I see two extremes in leadership. The first is that unspiritual and unloving men have been added to the leadership in local churches and have led in that direction.

The other extreme is that we find a "super spiritual" person and place that person in the position of leader. There may not even be a hint of a gift of leadership but here they are leading a church without God's gifting. It is easy for these super spiritual leaders to flounder and struggle so much that they lose their spirituality and end up discouraged and disgruntled. *"For by the grace given to me I say to every one of you: Do not think of yourself more highly than you ought, but rather think of yourself with sober judgment, in accordance with the measure of faith God has given you ... We have different gifts according to the grace given us ... If it is leadership, let him govern diligently; if it is showing mercy, let him do it cheerfully"* (Romans 12:3-8).

A church leader should *"set his heart on being an overseer"* but *"they must first be tested; and then if there is nothing against them, let them serve as deacons"* (1 Timothy 3:1, 10). There seems to be a sense of charge in Paul's instruction to Timothy: *"do not neglect your gift which was given you through a prophetic message when the body of elders laid their hands on you"* (1 Timothy 4:14). It is important to Paul that leaders not select other leaders too hastily. *"Do not be hasty in the laying on of hands"* (1 Timothy 5:22). Paul ever reminds Timothy that he is *"to fan into flame the gift of God, which is in you through the laying on of my hands"* (2 Timothy 1:6). This principle can lead to boldness and love in a balance that leaders can use to help others find the gifts that God has given them to serve in the kingdom. *"For God did not give us a spirit of timidity, but a spirit of power, of love and of self-discipline"* (2 Timothy 1:7).

After studying leadership for a lot of years, I am convinced that good leaders emerge slowly and deliberately from a group of believers who want to be God's church in the midst of a crooked and often perverse generation. As one looks at the first century church, it seems to me that leaders grew out of the daily work that was carried on. These natural leaders would come to the top and additional leadership training would be given to them by leaders who needed to move on to others who could be trained for service. *"And the things you have heard me say in the presence of many witnesses entrust to reliable men who will also be qualified to teach others"* (2 Timothy 2:2).

This is the way good leaders are usually trained—on the job! They watch and observe others as they do their work. They then work closely under the careful supervision of these leaders, and before long they acquire the skills to use the gifts God has given them. It seems strange that internships have only caught on in the last few years and mostly in the area of youth ministry.

There is another point I wish to make before leaving this area. As I have observed how leaders come to the top and become effective, it only happens with the permission of the group. In studying "Group Dynamics" and teaching it for a number of years, I have learned that groups often select their leaders as natural leaders emerge from within the group. It is only by permission that leaders begin to lead. Allowing the group the freedom to assent to this process will bring the best to leadership positions in the local church as well.

Ex Officio or De Facto?

I might here discuss the difference between *ex officio* leaders and *de facto* leaders. These Latin phrases say that there are often leaders who are the appointed official leaders but in fact others are the real leaders. You can often see this in local churches, and it needs to be recognized or you will find yourself being in good with the official leaders and kicked out by the *de facto* leaders. The *de facto* leader could be the wife, son, or friend of the *ex officio* leader. Many of you readers can give an example of the real power coming from someone behind the scenes (*de facto*) rather than from the appointed leaders (*ex officio*).

I have always been fascinated with power structures in local churches. We don't want to accuse local leaders of "playing politics" but they often do. When we are ignorant of the local power structures we can often miscalculate and reap a whirlwind of confusion and heartache. Even though all of us might agree that this scenario is not to be tolerated in Christ's body, we would probably agree that we have seen this diabolical nature at work.

I'm not really suggesting ways to change this but

suggesting that we all think it through. By following the major theme of this book—developing Christian leaders—we can avoid both the devastation that can destroy people who have the gift of leadership and the heartache of frustration as well.

Jesus has some very potent words about leadership as he speaks in Mark 10:43-45. The *"not so with you"* and the *"instead"* make it clear that in his church there is to be a style of leadership that differs from what the ways of the world and the ways of religious people of that day practiced. In a passage that speaks upside-down and rights the wrong, Jesus makes his way known and new.

Jesus bases leadership in his body on the will and the skill of meeting the group's needs. A servant mentality is looking at the needs of others and searching for ways of meeting those needs. Service is measured by the tasks we perform in meeting the needs of others in our group. There is a clear balance between the service we perform in tasks and the service we perform in relationships. We shall see that this balance is crucial to the ongoing leadership roles in the local church. How can I serve people in this church who are my brothers? What tasks can I do that will enhance them as God's children?

In fact, it is a truism that "he who meets needs, leads". Meeting both felt and real needs will make the local church a beehive of focused activity that will lead many to growth and will reach those who are searching.

We might be caught between a rock and a hard place when we throw this style of leadership alongside a passage like 1 Timothy 3:1. *"If anyone sets his heart on being an overseer, he desires a noble task."* Here it almost seems that a Christian should seek out leadership and lay out his qualifications for the church to judge and decide on the basis of his desire. I had a good man who was asked to serve as an elder of a local church who said he was not qualified because he did not "desire to be an overseer." He felt humbled and wondered how any humble person could seek such a position. I also saw the exact opposite where a person felt that one of the men who asked to be an elder should be rejected because he sought it.

You can see how developing balance is crucial to getting good leaders to serve. There is nothing immoral, illegal or fattening about the desire to be a leader. We don't want to make the role so difficult that no one will apply, and we don't want to make it so easy that anyone can step into such an important leadership role.

I want to be as practical as possible as we continue to look at how style of leadership is developed. I will do this by asking a series of questions that are intended to focus our thinking.

What are our goals?

What are our long and short term goals, because in every church there are **long and short term goals**. Long term goals will govern the local church over the long haul. These goals will determine the make-up of the church, its ministry leaders and the congregation's personality. Where do we want to be in five, ten and twenty years? What will leadership look like? What buildings must be planned for? What missions will we be doing in ten years? What staff ministries will need filling and where do we get them? We will need to ask the right questions of the right people if we are to get the needed information for good goals. Doing surveys of members has proven helpful in many churches.

Short term goals are of necessity under control of mission statements and long term goals. They are simply more immediate. Who are the teachers for the preschool? Who stays in contact with our mission people? How are we to expand our parking for next week's special service?

Short term goals must be monitored monthly, if not daily. Careful evaluation of the special service will help us to do it better next time and will cause us to ask tough questions about how it fits into our long term goals.

In the short term we need to evaluate each activity. For long term goals we must evaluate all programs and activities. I have found that the most difficult thing to get churches to do is to evaluate each program to see if it is meeting short and long term goals.

A church in the Midwest was losing members, and some of the most dedicated were backing away from leadership positions. After looking into their programs, it was apparent that several of their activities were draining their energy and time. Burnout was obvious. When we suggested that they carefully evaluate each activity we hit a roadblock. There were certain "sacred cows" that people are afraid to touch. "We have always done this, and we are not about to stop it." Although this church had several teachers teaching three times each week without any class for themselves, they were reluctant to look at any change. It was only after they had interviewed those who had backed away from leading that they were willing to admit they were attempting the impossible with their present membership.

Growing churches must examine every program and activity on a yearly basis if they are to keep the church focused and eliminate those activities that are as outdated as a buggy whip. Sacred cows can drain our energy and time from us, making us think we are doing something but we are only spinning our tires. We can spend lots of energy but experience no movement. It reminds me of a professor I had at the University of Nebraska who had to leave a Greek reading class early one day for a meeting of the Faculty Senate. His cynical comment as he left allowed us insight into how he felt about being on that body. "We sit and discuss whether we will spin the tires forward or backward." Before you laugh too hard, ask yourself if you have been in some of those meetings.

How much time and energy do we have?

The second question comes out of the first: **How much time and energy do we have?**

"I wish I had more time." Have you ever said that? If God had wanted you to have more time, He would have given you more. Many super-heroes have been dispatched to an early grave thinking that they had unlimited time and energy. I watched a team ministry trying to get going in a Midwestern town. Both families in the ministry were super-dedicated and wanted to succeed for the Lord. They would work for a week with little or no break, starting early and continuing until the wee hours of the morning. I noticed that after about a week of this around-the-clock performance, they would crash for about three days. They would either get sick or they would simply crash for lack of energy. It would then take about two weeks before they could go again at "capacity."

Working with them was a chore. However, after a few months of seeing that what they were doing was not accomplishing what they had hoped, they were willing to look at alternatives. "If you keep doing what you're doing, you'll keep getting what you're getting."

Burnout, including the cost of lost families and the loss of mental, spiritual and physical health, is still one of the most prevalent problems of church leaders. Spacing our activities and monitoring our lives will pay great dividends for leaders. We have limited time and energy and we need to learn to work smart and not just hard. Did not our Lord take time for himself and go to the mountains for a retreat?

Your style of leadership will be affected by time and energy. You only have so much given to you by God. Carefully use it, and don't think you are excused from the system because you are so dedicated.

How much do you care?

How much do you care? This is the third question that affects our style of leadership. Caring is a broad term that seems to get much ink in our modern world. From the care of endangered species to the care of homeless people, there is a constant bombardment for our time and our energy. Caring in the mode of a Mother Theresa certainly is needed in our world. When we make comparisons, we will often come up feeling guilty.

A leader's vertical relationship must increase so the horizontal relationships can grow. Loving God with our heart, soul, strength and might will turn over to a greater care for our neighbor. Is it possible for a person to care too much? I doubt it. I think what we think is caring might be an obsession rather than genuine.

Jesus was the most caring person who has ever loved, but he had time to go to a wedding, go fishing with his disciples, go to the mountain retreat and do other "mundane" things. Now when we care so much that we can't involve ourselves in the activities of family and friends, we probably don't care too much. We have an obsession and need to be treated for it.

Genuine caring will help us be involved in the whole life of our people. We may think we are "too spiritual" for the mundane things of life, but our example may not be Jesus for this. Keeping our focus might be helped if we would realize that our God is concerned about every aspect of life. Jesus could take time for children and relax as a woman washed his feet.

Having said that, our leadership style is still touched mightily by how much we care. Parts of the body are to *"have equal concern for each other"* (1 Corinthians 12:25). Paul felt *"daily the pressure of my concern for all the churches"* (2 Corinthians 11:28). *"Who is weak, and I do not feel weak? Who is led into sin, and I do not inwardly burn?"* (2 Corinthians 11:29). We need to be more like Timothy who *"takes a genuine interest"* in the welfare of others (Philippians 2:20).

Leaders who care enough to get into the abyss with men and women who are painfully struggling with sin rather than stand at the top in white robes spewing forth judgments in God's behalf are greatly needed in our churches. Leaders who have real empathy for the strugglers and can feel what they feel because they have been with them all the way are desperately needed in local churches. Caring enough to stay near the pain when running to the safety of church buildings is more inviting, can be seen by followers as real care and real concern. Followers who know that their leaders are not going to give up on them are inclined to keep on struggling.

What are our priorities?

Still limited by time and energy, leaders with care for others will **prioritize** so that the major amount of time and energy will be used in the best way. Leaders who find themselves running out of time and energy to do what is a top priority will probably find themselves bogged down in minutiae that tends to burn out good leaders.

Sit down and ask yourself what is your top priority. Make a list of all the things you want to accomplish as a leader this week. Divide these into A, B, C, and D. Now use these as your priority system for the week. Do the A's first and so on. Sit down at the end of the week and evaluate your week. What have you accomplished? Did you get engrossed in the C's and D's rather than finding delight in the things of most importance?

Although letting your people know that you care is important, setting them a balanced example is more lasting and will reap greater dividends. How can you lead where you refuse to go? Why are your people living daily in crisis? Why do leaders set the tone for management by crisis? When we find ourselves and others always in crisis, we might want to back away and look at our management principles. It is time that we show we care in ways that can lead people out of crisis and not contribute to their lapses.

What is our philosophy of leadership?

This is the next question that needs our attention. Philosophy of leadership will influence every aspect of our being. Our basic philosophy colors our attitude and attitude is everything. Here I might remind us that there is an individual philosophy and a group philosophy. The first influences the later but is never quite identical.

Our **leadership philosophy** will reveal how we view people. Do we let people take care of themselves or do we actively build community? This can sometimes depend upon the maturity level of the church, but also is affected by the way we think about people. Are we going to be hands-on kinds of leaders or do we move toward a more passive role? I will work on this concept in a later chapter but wanted to introduce it here for your reflection.

Wrestling with our own philosophy about leadership makes us ask questions concerning the biblical model and our own experiences. When we begin to study our local church, we will be influenced by our thinking patterns about the role of followers and the role of leaders. Do we allow members to find their own support structures or do we provide the structures? Does the model primarily build programs or people? Does our philosophy cause us to use people, abuse people or build up people? I have done some counseling for those who have been in abusive churches, and it is tough rowing. Our philosophy will cause us to work in the area of goal-oriented or people-oriented behaviors.

Programs and activities are influenced by our current belief systems and must fit into our value systems. Programs that provide structured support systems come from the heart of leaders who believe they know what is best for their people. On the other hand, if leaders expect the local people to find their own support system, they will allow the water of the local church to reach its own support level. There is much to say on both sides and some value in both systems.

What promotes maturity, commitment, and involvement?

This leads us to another question: What model best promotes genuine Christian maturity, commitment, and local church involvement? These are three goals that are inseparable.

No group of leaders would want to grow a local church that is too dependent on them and cannot make decisions on their own, or would they? Having Christians who are in the body for a period of time and are still being fed baby food is not our goal. Having to push baby Christians around in a stroller when they ought to be maturing is a pain and must not be tolerated in any local church. Leaders who lead in this way ought to learn God's way of maturing. *"Therefore let us leave the elementary teachings about Christ and go on to maturity"* (Hebrews 6:1).

Bottle-sucking Christians are not the goal of well-prepared leaders who *"have much to say about this, but it is hard to explain because you are slow to learn. In fact, though by this time you ought to be teachers, you need someone to teach you the elementary truths of God's word all over again"* (Hebrews 5:11-12). There is a point that all Christian must reach when they can have a little meat and get away from milk only. Leaders must match their philosophy with the teaching of the Word and what is best for maturing their followers. I have spent lots of time in mission churches and have found that this is a common malady. But it is too much a problem in older churches and must not be tolerated as leaders seek to *"equip the saints for the work of ministry, for building up the body of Christ"* (Ephesians 4:12, NRSV).

Two other questions need to be asked before we leave this area: 1) What are the benefits of the model you choose? 2) What is the cost? Here it is appropriate for us to ask ourselves just how the local church is fairing under our leadership model. What are some ways we could improve?

What one thing can we change that would make the most difference in the quality of the local church?

Discussion Questions

1. Discuss the leadership of Diotrephes in 3 John 9.

2. What was not "to be so" among Jesus' disciples? (Mark 10:43-45)

3. What has contributed towards the leadership void in some churches?

4. What one thing can we change that would make the most difference in your church?

5. Can you really choose a leadership style? Is it that simple?

Chapter 9
Committing Others to the Work

It is said that Paul and Barnabas "*had been committed to the grace of God for the work they had now completed*" (Acts 14:26). That must have been quite a day. They had been given a trust and had fulfilled it. "*While they were worshiping the Lord and fasting, the Holy Spirit said, 'Set apart for me Barnabas and Saul for the work to which I have called them.' So after they had fasted and prayed, they placed their hands on them and sent them off*" (Acts 13:2-3).

Paul would later write the Corinthians, "*Now it is required that those who have been given a trust must prove faithful*" (1 Corinthians. 4:2). How many times have we committed the work to others and never seen it brought to completion? Would it be presumptuous of me to say that this is a common occurrence in the local church?

Maybe there is a better way for us to commit others to the work than the way we are doing it. Could it be a flaw in the way we delegate that comes back to haunt us?

In 1987 Broadman Press published a book by Mark Short. *Time Management for Ministers* is now out of print, but to me is still a useful book. I will use some of the material from Chapter Six of Short's book. I have found this material to be helpful, and I trust that you will find it helpful to you.

What are the personal attributes that will help a leader when it comes time to commit others to the work? Although I have discussed the major concept in other places in this book, I want to say a few things about leadership in the crucial area of getting others to help in the local church. The principle of the church as a body (1 Corinthians 12) demands it.

Welcome Ideas

If we are to learn to commit the work to others **we must welcome other people's ideas**. We must be aware of our natural tendency to want to be the chief idea giver of the flock. Leaders can become jealous and defensive when another member suggests or develops an idea on his/her own. I have forgotten who originated the statement "You can accomplish almost anything if you don't care who gets the credit," but it is a good idea that works. There is more wisdom in many minds than in just a few.

Good leaders will develop idea shops in the local church and will usually sow a few seeds that others can water and let germinate. *"Where no counsel is, the people fall; but in the multitude of counselors there is safety"* (Proverbs 11:14, KJV). It is remarkable to see ideas really work in a church where leaders welcome people who have good ideas and are willing to make them work. It is a valid principle of good time management.

Accept Mistakes

If leaders are to learn to commit others to the work, they **must accept mistakes** on the part of others. When our small children are learning to involve themselves in new endeavors, we allow them ample room for mistakes. We do this because we are wise enough to know that errors can be valuable learning tools. If we do everything for the child, he will never learn to generate ideas for himself and will learn over-dependence. Parents who think they can do things better than the child will end up where they don't want to go. Leaders who refuse to accept the mistakes of others will end up in a time management debacle.

I am convinced that I have learned more by trial and error than from the reading of books or listening to others. From the pain of a mistake, lessons can be learned that can be learned in no other way. Leaders need to be there for their flock and accept the mistakes of others and guide them through to better decisions. What does the Bible mean when it talks about equipping *"the saints for the work of ministry, for the building up the body of Christ"*? (Ephesians 4:12, NRSV).

It becomes crucial when you must correct your child for a mistake. You must keep his self-image intact while helping him overcome the mistake. Losing your temper with the child can drive a wedge that will long remain after the event is forgotten. This is just as indispensable when we are faced with a member who has made a mistake or failed to complete his work.

Hold Your Temper

Keeping your **temper under control** is a must for church leaders. Terms like temperate, sensible, self-controlled, respectable and not violent but gentle, are extremely relevant with respect to leaders (see 1 Timothy 3:1-7).

The wise leader will find ways to affirm a brother who has failed in an assigned task. The brother has been willing to try a task, and he deserves affirmation for this. It is far better to have tried and failed than to have failed to try. It will do no good to chastise a brother and lose him to further work in the body. We might treat him as a smashed thumb and let the rest of the body come to his aid. It is also important that we lead in such a way that this brother does not fail in the next assigned work. As a father I recognize that a child has the right to be a child. *"When I was a child, I talked like a child, I thought like a child, I reasoned like a child"* (1 Corinthians 13:11). If we ever expect a brother to do better and mature, we will need to show acceptance and compassion when a mistake is made. There is enough perfectionism in the world; we don't need it in the church.

Learn When to Let Go

The final attribute for a leader is simply **learning when to supervise and when to let it go**. I will have more to say about this later, but here I want again to go for balance.

A good business manager knows when to step in and when to step out. A good leader knows when to look over the shoulder and when to back off. You will never be a delegating leader if you always feel that you could do the job better, quicker and more efficiently, and you step in to do the job. A smart leader is content to exercise open control over a project and its results. A smart leader does not tell a farmer how to plough, a carpenter how to drive nails, or a secretary how to type. Over-supervising will stunt the growth of gifted people and cause them to seek work elsewhere.

Here the sense of equilibrium will allow others to use their gifts and the leaders to use theirs. Finding the balance between too little and too much supervision is a task for smart leaders. Good people have been dispatched too early to the "members' retirement home for frustrated body parts" by too much or too little. Make clear assignments and expect and inspect, but never treat adult eyes as if they cannot see and ears as if they cannot hear.

Why do leaders have such trouble delegating? I have already suggested some of the reasons above. I have seen mothers who wish their daughters could learn to bake, but they know that they can do it better and quicker. Efficiency in the kitchen has to be learned.

Many fathers can't get their sons to mow the grass. Fathers can do it faster and better than a child. When my oldest son was five, he was holding the lower handle while I held the upper handle on the lawnmower. It took more time and more effort to finish the lawn. At eight, Keith was doing it himself, and I could go fishing.

Leaders fuss and fume about members who won't get involved. When we have equipped them as God has instructed, we might not have to fuss so much. Allowing members to develop as a body will make delegating much easier. You might want to accuse me of oversimplifying the problem, but I think there is a suggestion for a solution if you will look closely.

The leaders' love for trivial chores might get us out of trusting others with tasks that could free us for more shepherding. I may be writing with tongue in keyboard but there is a real point to make.

Why are leaders caught up in doing the trivial tasks of the body while never seeming to get on with the majors? Keeping the main thing the main thing is not easy business, but it could free us to let others function in the body. Someone has facetiously stated that shepherds do the deacons' work and the deacons are left out. I would say that both functions are hurting in this scenario.

There was a book written a few years ago by Charles Hummel called *The Tyranny of the Urgent*. How many of us have been tyrannized by the urgent? Dr. W.B. West was a beloved professor at Harding Graduate University School of Religion. I can't remember how many times I sat in his classes and heard him say, "Do not neglect the important for the necessary." It took a while for that remark to come clear to me.

> **Notes from Nanny**
> The things we want to do are often never done because we feel we don't have the time to do them.
> Many deeds are never performed because in the hurry of daily life we think there is not time to perform the intended acts of kindness.
> The world would be a better place if those who say "I don't have time," altered their schedules and did some of the things they know they should and really want to do.
> Take time to be yourself; you cannot successfully be another. Do you find yourself never getting to do the things you want to do because there is no time or energy?

As I was writing this section, I stopped to read a bulletin that I get each week. Craig Shelton's Youth Article in the Centerville, Tennessee, bulletin had an article called "Notes From Nanny."

There is also the ever-recurring **issue of control**. I am now treading on thin ice, but I feel that our thinking might need a challenge in this area. Could it be that one of the reasons we don't assign more tasks to our people is that we are concerned about who is in charge?

I am not accusing us of being the sons of Zebedee and wanting to sit at places of authority in the kingdom, (see Mark 10:35ff.), but leaders can put a cap on the growth of the church by their leadership style. If they must be in charge of every program and know all the "ins and the outs" of each work, the cap is on. There are only so many hours in the day and so much energy to expend. When that energy is going into too much supervision for control of the church, there is precious little left for quality shepherding.

Leaders who just want to do it themselves can avoid the hassle of dealing with people. The sheep make too many "baa's" and have an awful smell, so let's not spend so much time in the sheepfold.

There are problems when the leaders get into the pasture and get their hands smelling like sheep, but when this is not done, the sheep never learn to carry their own weight. Imagine leaders who are not afraid of the hassles that come with working with sheep, and they are constantly dealing with those who are growing and maturing. They can learn to trust the sheep and commit a trust to them.

It is hard work to instruct another. It is less work to do it myself. There is even the prevailing feeling that if you want a job done right, you better do it yourself. Spending time planning and preparing for equipping can be hard, but in the long run we want our people to develop their gifts and talents and become leaders for the church of tomorrow. Sure it is tough work teaching a child to fish, but it is better than giving him the fish and making him dependent on you for the rest of his life.

I have a pond in the front of my house. It has several bass, bluegill, and a few catfish in it. The rule for fishing in the pond is that "All adults must be accompanied by a child." Several children in the area have gotten their start in fishing in this pond. There is an electric line across the pond, and if one is not careful he will lose his lure by wrapping the fishing line around the electric line. I have watched fathers who continue to warn their youngsters about the line as they demonstrate the proper way to cast the line.

Adults, if you actually want to fish, don't bring your kids. The adult's job with kids is to instruct, teach, and untangle the line. Would there be a lesson there for church leaders? We might have more fishers of men if we were unafraid to roll up our sleeves and untangle a few lines and teach our flock how to bait a hook. The difficulty of instruction is outweighed when we look for the goal and purpose of leadership.

If we are totally honest, we can learn to admit that others might discover that they can get along without us. Well, whoopee!

Some leaders in churches fear that if I delegate too much, others might think that I'm not doing my work. Some may even look at delegation as an admission of weakness. I would argue the exact opposite. When you delegate and commit a trust to another, you are displaying strength.

Mark Short has a short quiz that will test your ability to delegate. Take it and expand the attitude and approach in your own ministry.

Testing Your Ability to Delegate

On the next page, circle the number that most nearly matches your true feelings. Please don't answer the way you think you should. The test is only as helpful as you make it.

(1) strongly disagree (2) disagree (3) agree (4) strongly agree

1. The church expects me to know all the details of the operation.	1 2 3 4
2. I think my church expects me to attend all committee meetings.	1 2 3 4
3. The church leaders never seem to get the work done the way I want it.	1 2 3 4
4. Delegation takes too much time.	1 2 3 4
5. Church workers can do routine tasks, but I must care for non-routine matters.	1 2 3 4
6. I work longer hours than I should.	1 2 3 4
7. Church leaders do not have my level of commitment.	1 2 3 4
8. If I delegated more, I would lose some of the enjoyment of my job.	1 2 3 4
9. When I give someone a job, I detail explicit instructions for that job.	1 2 3 4
10. When I delegate, I often have to do the job over when the person responsible drops the ball.	1 2 3 4
11. My people are not experienced enough to do the work.	1 2 3 4
12. I get upset when they show incompetence.	1 2 3 4
13. To delegate is to lose control.	1 2 3 4
14. I don't mind delegating if I'm given the opportunities to review and veto.	1 2 3 4
15. I like to view the work in such a way that I can input at each progression.	1 2 3 4
16. I tend to be a perfectionist.	1 2 3 4

TOTAL SCORE: _____

(add the numbers you have circled)

Your Delegation Rank:
46 - 64   You probably have a serious problem in delegation
36 - 45   Your delegation habits could be improved.
26 - 35   You have some room to grow
16 – 25   You are a superior delegator

See Short, Mark: *Time Management for Ministers.* Pp. 74 – 75. Broadman Press: Nashville, Tenn.; 1987.

Discussion Questions

1. What can you do about your personal objections to delegation?

2. What can delegation do for your ministry?

3. Has your temper ever hurt your ministry? How?

Chapter 10
Leadership Styles

Finding a Style

When one argues for balance in ministry, he usually meets with good response. The real problem comes when you try to be consistent and find practical ways to implement balance.

This, and the following chapter, might be the most difficult chapters to write. It is hoped that these chapters can be the most helpful of the book. What I want to accomplish is a thorough look at leadership styles that can be most helpful to church leaders in the twenty-first century. At the same time, I want to find the Biblical principles that can guide us to a more balanced approach to leadership in today's church.

I did a seminar a few years ago on Leadership and called it "Leadership that is Biblical and that Works." It didn't sound right to me, so I later changed the title. I am still looking for a good title for this chapter and I hope that someone might suggest one before the next revision of this book. What I plan to do is to use a grid and allow it to shed light on the styles that might be needed in our present condition. I also intend to show that it is, indisputably, the model that we find in Scripture. With that chore in mind I ask for a careful perusal of these principles.

Some of our readers are not familiar with the use of the grid. The explanation that I will give is not from an expert but I know of no better way to show how leadership works than to use the grid.

The grid has two axes. One is vertical, and the other is horizontal. I will use the horizontal axis as X and the vertical as Y. The vertical axis will be used to show the leader's concern for people – Shepherding. The horizontal axis will be used to show the leader's concern for form and order – "Bishoping" or "Overseeing". Observe the first grid with the axis X showing the concern for people–Pastors/Shepherds and the Y showing the concern for form–bishops/overseers.

The grid goes from 0-9 both vertically and horizontally.

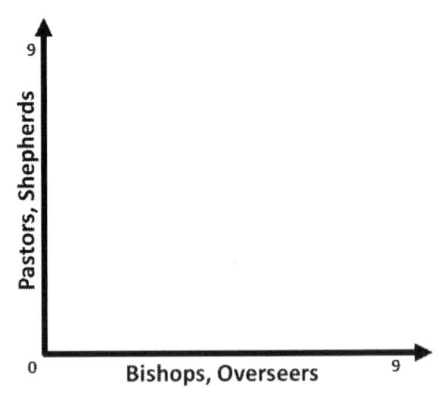

(Graph: Y-axis labeled "Pastors, Shepherds" from 0 to 9; X-axis labeled "Bishops, Overseers" from 0 to 9)

When a leader is a (9, 0), the grid shows that he is concerned with form and order with little or no concern for people. Perhaps we could say that the New Testament Pharisee fit here on the grid.

On the other hand if a leader is a (0, 9), he has high concern for people with little concern for form—rules and regulations. This type of leader would throw out the clear rules for the Christian to hold on to the person of interest. While the (9, 0) would trash the people for the principle, the (0, 9) would trash the principle for the people.

The vertical axis is used in this book to illustrate the interest in people—*poimeen*—while the horizontal axis illustrates the concern for principle–*episkopos*. Multiple leaders in a local church could have a better balance than just one leader could have as a single. This could be the reason the Bible seems to always address elders/overseers/shepherds in the plural.

It would be perfectly ideal to have all leaders in a local church as (9, 9) but we don't live in a perfect world and most of us recognize our own inadequacies. Only Jesus was a perfect (9, 9). He was the only one who spoke the truth in love perfectly. This does not mean that we give up trying. All leaders should reach as high as possible in following the example of the builder of the church.

There is one other thing that will be helpful to you as you study this grid. Through the years I have asked people attending my seminars on leadership to draw their understandings of what each leadership style looks like to them. The drawing and the grid are placed alongside each other to let the reader study them together. It will be necessary for the reader to study both the grid and the drawing of the movement within the grid discussed in the text.

I hope the reader is now ready to launch into a thorough study of leadership that is both biblical and dynamic. The biggest room in anybody's house is the room for improvement so let's get on with the improving.

Study carefully the figures that are in this chapter and follow the thrust of each style. These figures are the result of several years of presenting these principles and asking participants to draw their concepts of the styles. I have selected one drawing for each style and I hope that a picture will form in your mind.

Leadership Style One: Laissez-faire (1, 1)

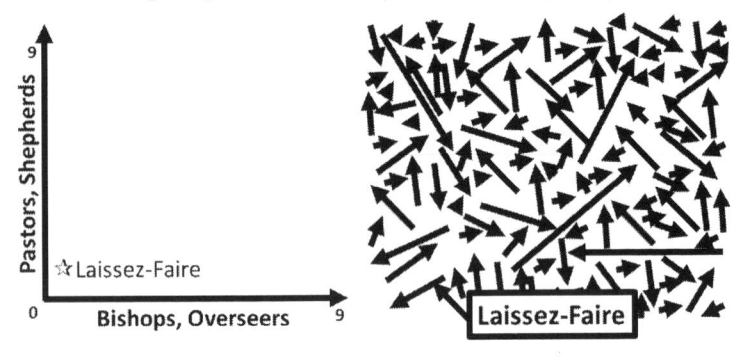

I understand that some cynically call this style of leadership "Lazy-Fair." But we must understand that this genre of leadership can serve good and noble purposes. It is a **permissive and passive form of leadership**, and although it will not work best in every situation, it still needs a fair hearing. (Note the 1, 1 position on the grid.)

Following are several characteristics of this type of leadership and how they might enhance our management in the local church. Laissez-faire leadership style is minimal control with members directing. It definitely is a bottom-up approach to leading a local church. It works well when the members are fairly functional and able to carry on the necessary activities to keep the church moving toward some desired goal. This style of leadership works best in small family churches.

Back in 1984, Lyle Schaller wrote a book about the awkward sized church. He noted the characteristics of three church sizes:

Small Church	1 - 100
Middle-Sized Church	100 – 200
Large Church	200+

I think that it is in the small church that the laissez-faire style will work best. However, I am not prepared to say that this only works in smaller churches. At times it may work well in larger groups, as I will attempt to show later in this chapter.

In the small church the power seems to reside in key families and operates like a participatory democracy. Occasionally there will be a congregational meeting to decide critical points, and the leading families will be the dominant responders. The preacher will be more of an enabler. He will be in tune with the primary group and the opinion-maker of the church. This church, operating like one big happy family, will be people-focused.

In Laissez-Faire churches, there is little preparation for things to happen. Things are usually left to drift, and what needs doing will usually be done. It may look as if there is no concern and care in this leadership style. This is simply not true. This is a people-oriented leadership style, and the concern will come out as it does in a family.

Unfortunately this leadership style doesn't accomplish a great deal beyond maintenance. Apart from the necessary items that must happen on Sunday and during the week, there is little organized activity going on. Other than social amenities that control the family atmosphere, there is a notable lack of discipline. This can sometimes encourage fragmentation.

In churches where this style of leadership is apparent, there will be little attempt to appraise or regulate events. Decisive plans are usually not made and everybody is happy as long as the heat is working in February.

Notice where this type of leadership fits on the grid and how several have drawn this style in our seminars:

Leadership Style Two: Autocratic (9, 1)

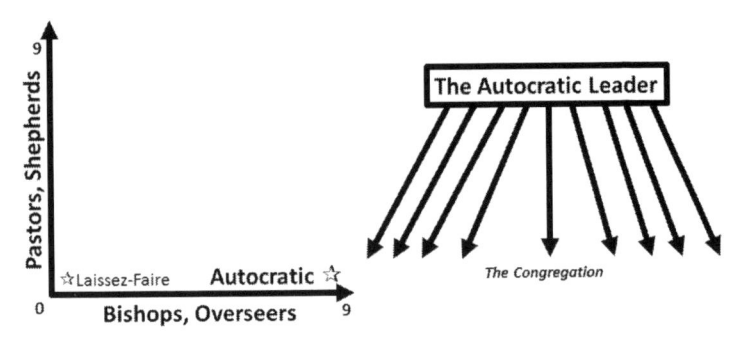

There is a temperament known as the Choleric. This temperament expresses **a high need to be in control**. This leadership style tends to be domineering and sometimes dictatorial. As I have said several times in this book, there are times when a strong hand is necessary to quell chaos.

"When the country is in chaos, everybody has a plan to fix it - but it takes a leader of real understanding to straighten things out" (Proverbs 28:2, The Message).

The Autocratic Leader takes total control with members of the group as listeners and followers. I am told that when the paramedics arrive, they have complete control of a medical emergency. A friend of mine recently told of an accident where a doctor was on hand and had begun medical treatment when the paramedics arrived. The doctor stepped back and allowed the paramedics to take charge. Later, I was told that by law the paramedics are in complete control of a medical situation and that other emergency personnel must allow them to do their job. I don't know if this is totally true in any given situation, but it is a good illustration of this leadership style. Later, I want to make a point that in some situations it is a necessity for an autocratic leader to take loving and understanding charge of situations that demand strong and decisive action.

The Autocratic Leader will be the chief person in the local church to determine goals and policies. It is the nature of the Autocratic leader to take control, and his influence will be felt in all parts of the organization. In some ways this leader has the entrepreneurial spirit. He is great at founding and planting churches. Early policies and goals are his forte.

When things are in chaos, this leader functions as a trouble shooter and will take the necessary lead in getting the problems solved and the church moving. This style of leader is a fix-it person. When a task needs doing, this leader will tackle it with vim and gusto and will cherish every minute of the challenge.

Because of this person's gifts, he is interested in content more than people. (Note the 9, 1 position on the grid.) Getting on with the task is of utmost importance. He will need to be more aggressive and maybe a bit more confrontational. There will be a need for lots of decision-making to insure the ongoing operation. This leader will not retreat or hesitate when a tough decision has to be made. Since he is more interested in content than people, he will sometimes march through sacred ground and leave a lot of injured body parts strewn about.

The Autocratic Leader makes decisions regardless of other views. In fact, this leader will not consult others in most situations. Perhaps here we can note a weakness in this style of leadership, even while saying that, in some circumstances, this leader comes in handy. There is little doubt what the decision is, and it is usually clear where this person is going. His decision making power is one strength that he lives and dies by. He makes a decision and then never questions it. Since he has not consulted others in the decision, he will not consult them in revision or in carrying it out. He may even ride roughshod over others' feelings and push aside their gifts. This leader will not be able to lead in the long haul, because once the chaos has passed and some sense of normalcy is restored, this leader will find that he is a dinosaur about to become extinct.

This style of leader usually talks too much and asks and

answers his own questions. In a meeting this leader will ask a question and make a proposal to get the proposal moving. Even if others are permitted to answer, their answers will not be considered unless they have been part of his already decided agenda. He might surround himself with "yes" men and use them as power devices to help him accomplish his agenda. For him, the goal is of utmost importance, and he needs authority and backing to reach that goal.

Because of the nature of this style of leader, he will need to focus attention on himself. Without the attention, he will be unable to accomplish the task, so he will need to be sure that he has the attention of all the followers. He is the general, and all eyes must be on him while all ears listen for the next command.

Finally, this leader will need to be good at pulling strings as though others were like puppets. He will study the power structures and use the ones he can and attempt to negate the rest. People who can't be controlled are usually dispatched quickly or relegated to non-influential positions. Most gifted leaders will leave unless they want constantly to fight for a hearing. The long-range problem is that the best leaders in other categories might be driven away. Soon there is no longer a need for the trouble shooter, but there will not be good leaders left behind to get on with the building up of the body of Christ.

You might get the impression that I am not much in favor of this leader. But I do understand that sometimes exerted power is necessary to preserve the body. In international situations, it is sometimes necessary to be more aggressive than the aggressor. This is true in the local church as well. In the long run I believe that this style of leadership will need to be replaced with a better balance. But sometimes the good of the local body makes it necessary to *"Obey your leaders and submit to their authority. They keep watch over you as men who must give an account. Obey them so that their work will be a joy, not a burden, for that would be no advantage to you"* (Hebrews 13:17).

Leadership Style Three: Authoritative (7, 3)

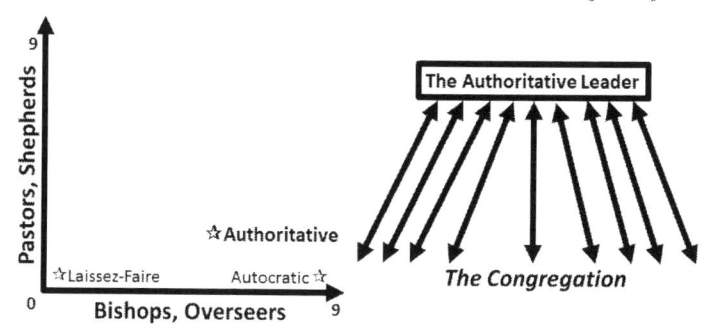

There are some who would combine this style with the previous one. I think that there is not only a subtle difference but a real distinction. Whereas Autocratic Leaders are aggressive and dominant, Authoritative Leaders are **definite, yet responsive.** Notice the emphasis on the responsive. They may look alike at times, but the key to understanding this leadership style is in the word responsive. He is attentive to the thinking of others and will be attempting to be more agreeable. He has moved more in the direction of shepherding and has taken a step back from overseeing.

The Authoritative Leader will be more accepting of others' views and feelings and will lead in ways that are more accommodating. He will appear to be compliant and conciliatory as he will go out of his way to solicit opinions of other members of the group. He will be definite, but he will yield when the need is great.

The Authoritative Leader will be strong on control with members actively involved in the discussion. You will know who is in charge but will appreciate the fact that you have been heard. Since opinions of others are valued, most of the followers will feel that they have been given a fair hearing.

You can see that this leader has a definite purpose and plan but is not isolated to the extent that he is closed to modification. Even though he might think that his plans are the best, he will stop and listen and will modify those plans.

He would have a tough time doing a complete turnaround. As he takes into consideration the alternate opinions of others, he will fight for his way but be flexible enough to alter those plans to accommodate opposing ideas.

This style of leader will definitely be recognized as an opinion maker and dynamic leader. He will be active and energetic but will seek the activity of others. These leaders are a delight to have on board because they accomplish much without ruffling lots of feathers. Since there is continuing communication between this leader and the flock, there will be less likelihood that strong feelings will turn into diabolical conflict. Some members don't have to have their way; they just have to have their say. This leader will be a better listener than the Autocratic leader and most will feel that they have been heard.

This leadership style has more balance than the autocratic model. These leaders are prepared to give strong direction and support as needed. There will be little doubt where these want to lead, but the balance comes as they are willing to be supportive of what others are doing. They are not just about being on their own soapbox and jerking others over to their position. They are right alongside others giving support easily and quickly.

This style is not about domination, but will be very persuasive. You will seldom find manipulation here as you might expect to find in the Autocratic style. The authoritative leaders will use communication skills to involve others. Persuasion will dominate, while coercion, compulsion, and brainwashing will be rejected. Force and intimidation will give way to talking things out, and the party spirit is less likely to creep from the woodwork. Notice the arrows that go in both directions in the figure below, and the congregation is more prominent.

Leadership Style Four: Democratic (5, 5)

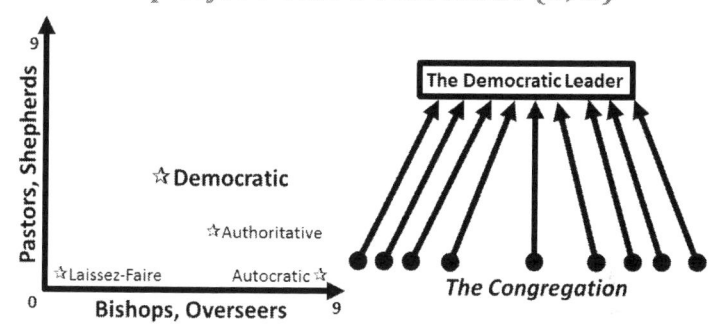

The Democratic style of leadership is **group-centered**. The will of the majority will prevail. This seems to be a good style for most westerners but sometimes runs into rough sledding in other parts of the world. It has not always worked efficiently but has been productive of long-lasting good. As you notice the characteristics of the democratic style of leadership, you will want to think carefully about how this approach works in your local church.

The first characteristic of the democratic leader is the concept of shared control. Meetings are run on the basis of consensus. Each person is heard, and each person gets a vote. Usually there is some agreement on how consensus works and what constitutes a majority. People are brought on board by persuasion, not manipulation. Information and feelings hold equal sway, and the meeting is run by "Robert's Rules of Order."

It is the group that holds the power, and the responsibility is shared. There is no one person who will dominate and domineer. It's one for all and all for one. Details are worked out for the best interests of the majority and the leadership is coming and going from the group not from an individual. The group serves as the focus for leadership. There might be one leader who is more dominant, but it will always be the group that holds the power. Power is not in the hands of a few but emanates from the combined caucus. This style of leadership must be based on a firm faith in other people. Without this trust of others, the group will resort to power struggles, and disagreements will be activated and heightened. During meetings there is an emphasis on sharing information. I have often heard: "A democracy can't remain if the constituents remain in ignorance." It is not so crucial that all members are in agreement, but that all have their say. Once we have had our say, we are more willing to accept the best judgments of the majority.

Democratic Leaders create a sense of security and belonging. Following a visit with a former member, with whom I had met on several occasions, I attempted to extract reasons for his turning away and not continuing his involvement, he finally said, "I just never felt like I belonged."

Why is it that lots of our followers never seem to feel secure in their relationships in the local church? Could it be because they have never been given opportunity to have their say and feel that they have been heard? There may be something about the democratic process that allows for feelings of security to permeate an organization so that *"if one part suffers, every part suffers with it; and if one part is honored, every part rejoices with it"* (1 Corinthians. 12:26).

There is nothing that will help more to keep local members deep in involvement than the feeling of belonging. I am not saying that the leadership style that is more democratic can accomplish this alone but that there is a definite contribution that can be made by allowing all members to hear and be heard. Win Arn has shown from his research that unless there is a feeling of belonging there is very little likelihood of continuing involvement. Feelings of loving and being loved can be encouraged as democratic leaders lead the local church into involvement that fosters feelings of security and belonging.

"Nobody at that church ever listens" is not usually heard in churches where leaders lead democratically. We often hear politicians mouth the thought that all constituents will be heard. I doubt that this is the absolute case in politics or in church leadership, but it is a worthy goal. Democratic leadership style sees that the group discusses all policies. Providing means to reach this worthy goal is a leadership challenge. Present structures may or may not be designed to accomplish this goal. If this is not the case there will be a need for some restructuring so that all members are heard and made to feel secure.

It might be atypical in your church to rethink your structures and build in opportunities for more interaction, but it might pay good dividends as you look to the future. We are not governed by the majority rule but by the Sovereign rule of God. Yet, in areas where there is no "thus says the Lord," we would do our churches a favor by developing a more interactive model of church leadership.

When this democratic leadership style is used, you will find that other leaders are naturally developed. If we could insure that others have a chance to lead, we would see a different type of leader being developed in the local church. More could be equipped *"for works of service, so that the body of Christ may be built up"* (Ephesians 4:12).

I wonder why leaders are not developed in the church as they are in business. Much on-the-job training goes into making a good leader in the world of business. Are we doing any on-the-job training in the church, or does our present structure prevent others from learning to lead by leading?

I sometimes sadly reflect on the lack of leaders in some churches. I see people who attend churches and are dynamic leaders in their business and community. Why are they not used in this capacity in the local church? Are we using the gifts of our people as well as or better than business and community?

Giving other's the chance to lead is part of the democratic leadership style. We would do well to integrate more of this in our local churches. One of the strong suits for the democratic leadership style is that as we allow for leadership and provide more chances for others to lead, we have leaders coming on to replace the ones who leave. If a leader withdraws, the group will not fall apart.

There was a church in the upper Midwest that had made remarkable growth for several years. The local leader was on fire and built a solid growth chart. Within a year after he resigned, the church had lost more than half of the 800 people in attendance, and within another year it had almost closed its doors. No leaders came to the front to help this church move ahead because none had ever had the opportunity to lead. Tragedy awaits a church where there is no intentional leadership training administered by using people on the job, giving them the chance to lead.

Put your finger in a bowl of water and pull it out. Where did the hole go that had been created by your finger? Now think about your local church. What happens when a leader withdraws? When the leader is gone, will there be leaders that rush in to fill the hole?

I was just in a meeting with our involvement minister. As we talked about an upcoming ministry leaders' meeting, he said that he wanted to have the ministry leaders dream dreams about their area of work. In the democratic leadership style others are empowered to plan and execute ministries. This bottom-up approach has been discussed elsewhere but needs to be inserted here as well. Lack of ideas will discourage the authoritarian leader; but that same lack should encourage the democratic leader.

Stimulating ideas come from a stimulating environment. Leaders who can challenge others to plan and execute ministries will find there will never be a dearth of new ministries waiting to carry the torch to the community and beyond.

Leadership Style Five: Rapport (1, 9)

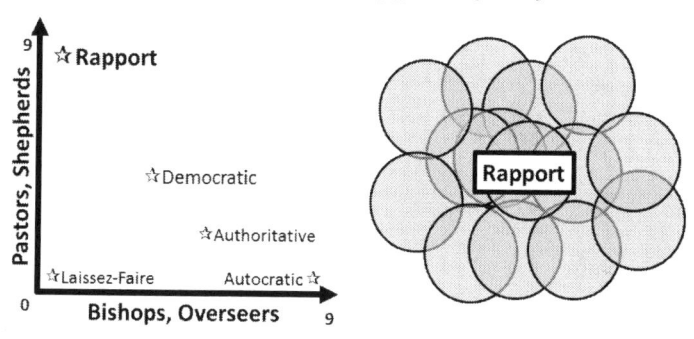

If a leader is strongly oriented toward people, he will be strong in the pastoring area. We call this leadership style Rapport. This style is **strong in shepherding and will look for agreement in most situations**. A leader in the area of Rapport will want to know what everybody thinks and wants. He will not move against people and will use every means to see that all people get what they want.

Here is where the chaos happens. There is little organization and supervision. All programs are run as efforts to keep the people in good spiritual form. Leaders serve as enablers. All are part of a team and leaders are coaches for spiritual harmony. Programs are set into operations to meet a specific felt or real need of people, but there is little care given that things happen as they should. This means that there will be a good show of planning programs, but little accomplished because there is little accountability.

There is a big difference between enablers and equippers. Rapport leaders allow people to do their own thing and therefore programs will probably not get done. Equippers will challenge and help people do their work and see that there is accountability.

This leadership style certainly has some good characteristics. It is people focused and love motivated. People will feel loved in this church and there will be some loyalty. But there will also be a mild underlying frustration because there will be few programs that are sustained because of lack of organization and supervision. Some churches can thrive on this type of leadership but these will be few and far between.

An example of this style of leadership happened in a church in the Midwest. There was a family there who thought that their son was a good leader in the singing of hymns, but he had some detracting habits and could not lead the congregation. The leaders didn't want to offend anyone so they offended everyone. That's the chaos that can result from seeking Rapport at the expense of wisdom.

The next style of leadership I will reserve for the next chapter. There I will attempt to tie all of these styles together and suggest how they can all be used in the local church for God's body to be *"joined and held together by every supporting ligament, grows and builds itself up in love, as each part does its work"* (Ephesians 4:16).

Discussion Questions

1. Which style of leadership is dominant in your congregation?

2. When is laissez-faire the best?

3. What styles of leadership would be more optimal for your congregation?

4. Make a chart listing the leadership styles along with pros and cons of each.

Chapter 11
A New Old Style of Leadership

A "Third Way"

Spend a little time restudying the grid at the beginning of Chapter 10. Notice that the two sides of the grid have to do with two words used in the Greek language of the New Testament. The Biblical terms overseer and pastor are generally used interchangeably in the English New Testament. These terms refer to the spiritual leaders who are primarily responsible for preaching-teaching, shepherding, and supervising.

Episkopos (επίσκοπος) is the term referring to supervision. The word literally means "one who looks over." It is sometimes translated in the older versions of the English Bible as Bishop. *Poimen* (ποιμήν) is the term for pastor. Its primary meaning has to do with shepherding the flock. I place these on the opposite sides of the grid to point out that their orientation is different. Overseers are the goal-oriented leaders who wish to get on with the job at hand. Shepherds are those who are closely identified with the people and want to be there for them in all situations.

As you study the grid, don't automatically conclude that these terms are mutually exclusive. Though overseers are more the Authoritarian (7, 3), they are likely to have other orientations as well. Shepherds are most likely to seek rapport (1, 9) and be people focused, but they will have goals and plans for the flock as well. Our goal is to achieve a balance capable of leading a healthy church.

A colleague recently asked me about my approach to

counseling. "Are you a cognitive therapist or a behavioral therapist?" After listing other theories of counseling, she answered her own question. She smiled and said that I was probably an eclectic therapist. Eclectic means multifaceted, many-sided, complex, discriminating.

What she meant was that the method that I used aimed to discern the specific needs of a client and to proceed on that basis. No one method will work in every situation and counselors will most likely use methods that are in harmony with their basic philosophy while meeting the needs of the person seeking direction.

This leads us to the term **Maieutic**. Definitions might vary from one dictionary to another; some of you won't find it in your dictionary. The American Heritage Dictionary gives a good meaning: "Of or relating to the aspect of the Socratic method that induces a person to bring forth latent concepts through a logical sequence of questions." It is an old term for **midwife**. I believe that church leaders should be midwives.

What do you get when you cross an *episkopos* with a *poimeen*? You get a midwife. What does a good shepherd do? He asks logical question to bring forth latent concepts to help him learn the real needs of his sheep. Only by taking the right approach can he begin to help the member of his flock to find answers to his questions.

Think about it for a moment. What do good midwives do? They come close and observe the status of the woman in labor. Through observation they can begin to know the real condition of the client. It will be at this point that the midwife will make decisions about the care and keeping of this individual. Does the midwife take charge or allow things to progress naturally? In a circumstance that requires a lot of intervention, the midwife will become authoritarian. If things are moving more smoothly, the Maieutic leader will shepherd, but with less involvement. She will become a rapport leader.

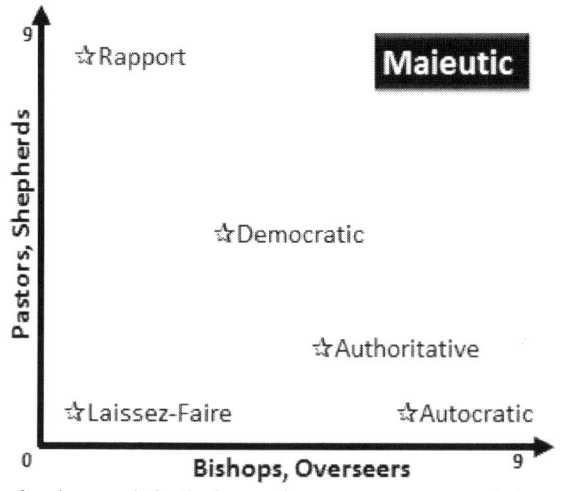

```
                    9|
                     |  ☆Rapport              ┌─────────┐
                     |                        │ Maieutic│
                     |                        └─────────┘
       Pastors, Shepherds
                     |
                     |         ☆Democratic
                     |
                     |                ☆Authoritative
                     |
                     |  ☆Laissez-Faire      ☆Autocratic
                    0|_____→
                                Bishops, Overseers         9
```

Developing a right balance between too much intervening and too little is learned over years of training and practice. Church leaders must never take over what only the member can do. But all leaders must be ready to intervene quickly and decisively as the occasion dictates. Knowing when to take a more active part and when to be more laid back is something that comes through wisdom and years of leading. Maieutic leaders can begin to respect the sheep and be there to take the lead when it is required. They can also respect the sheep enough to let them do things for themselves when this is called for.

Leaders who do not learn this lesson well will develop weak, acquiescing people who will never learn to develop as God desires, and they will end up wanting to be pushed about in a stroller and fed baby food for too long. Leaders who learn this lesson well can have the privilege of leading mature, thinking, and contributing Christians. Maieutic leaders, with tender hearts and Christ-like care, can develop a holistic approach toward the flock that will allow intervention and non-intervention as needed.

Characteristics of Maieutic Leaders

The characteristics of Maieutic leaders allow us to see the dynamics of leadership in its Biblical fullness. As we look at these characteristics individually, we can apply the information and become better leaders.

Characteristic One

The Maieutic Leader exercises **strong control, shared control, or minimal control, as needed**.

Some situations demand that leaders move in, move fast, and move decisively. The apostle Paul was not about to back down on a principle when Peter seemed more willing to give than to stand. *"When Peter came to Antioch, I opposed him to his face, because he was in the wrong...when I saw that they were not acting in line with the truth of the gospel"* (Galatians 2:11, 14).

It is clear that there are times when leaders must step to the front and take charge of given situations to make sure that truth is not sacrificed at the price of a relationship. It is always appropriate for leaders to *"contend for the faith that God has once for all entrusted to the saints"* (Jude 3). Maieutic leaders, like midwives, will step in and be sure that the nine months of carrying a baby are not ruined at the point of delivery. *"Watch out that you do not lose what you have worked for, but that you may be rewarded fully"* (2 John 8).

Leaders must continually ask God for wisdom (James 1:5) to make proper decisions in every situation. Is this a situation that requires minimal control or strong control? Minimum control requires that leaders have confidence in those who are following. *"I have great confidence in you; I take great pride in you. I am greatly encouraged; in all our troubles my joy knows no bounds. . . . I am glad I can have complete confidence in you"* (2 Corinthians 7:4, 16).

Sharing control is a democratic style of leadership. Many are the times that leaders need only to be there and help as the plan unfolds and new life is added to the local body. When you combine the qualities of overseer with those of pastor, you have a leader who takes control only when supervision is needed at the moment.

When nature is moving along as expected, the Maieutic leader can sit back and exercise minimal control. Overseer types have a difficult time with this because their nature is to Bishop. Over-control may need a bit of Rapport in the leadership to balance this need to be in charge. Perhaps that's the reason that you seem to have multiple leaders when elders are mentioned in the Scriptures. (If you are getting confused with these terms, go back and study the grid again.)

Characteristic Two

The Maieutic Leader **has definite, but adaptable plans**.

The leader with the orientation toward *episkopos* is the planner. He will want to see everything laid out clearly on paper, and he will go over and over the plan. He loves to plan, revise the plans, and see that they are carried out properly. He is a hands-on kind of leader and will see that things run smoothly.

It is hard work being a Bishop type. It is an honorable ambition to be an overseer (1 Timothy 3:1). It is also a respected leadership style. *"Now we ask you, brothers, to respect those who work hard among you, who are over you in the Lord and admonish you"* (1 Thessalonians 5:12). This hard-working individual will be likely to Manage by Objectives.

Because this leader is focused on objectives, he will help the church move from ideas to applications. Moving ideas through the process that can make them workable plans is what he is about. He will be adept at transforming nebulous Christian goals into accomplishable tasks.

The *poimeen* side of the Maieutic leader will be adaptable and people-focused. This side of the leader will promote cohesiveness and Christian fellowship. The shepherd leader will champion caring and the meeting of needs of the sheep. Ezekiel records the words of the Great Shepherd in chapter 34:8-10: *"Because my flock lacks a shepherd and so has been plundered ... and because my shepherds did not search for my flock but cared for themselves rather than the flock ... I will remove them from tending the flock."*

The Maieutic leader is no hireling. He is the real shepherd who fully owns his sheep (John 10:13). The uncaring shepherd is an anomaly. Whereas the overseer might come off as uncaring, and many in the flock might feel that "No one cares for my soul," the Maieutic leader combines these characteristics and genuinely cares for the physical, emotional, and spiritual welfare of the flock. There is a biblical balance in these leaders who can manage to have definite plans with willingness to adapt when necessary.

Characteristic Three

The Maieutic Leader **is active and energetic, but he seeks the activity of others**.

You can see the Maieutic leader-midwife who plans and sets goals but always listens to the needs of the flock. This leader will prepare for the time of delivery and be ready when the baby arrives. All is ready for the next meeting or the next event. All bases are covered, and the time will be planned for each item on the agenda.

But always, before the carrying out of the plans, the midwife-leader will check the action and the needs of the mother to be. Again the leader will seek the full involvement of the sheep in meeting their needs. There is an old saying: "You can lead a horse to water, but you can't make him drink." I know I have mixed metaphors, but the Maieutic leader will insist on the activity of others. Spiritual muscles grow strong by movement and activity. No Maieutic leader will be satisfied with couch-potato Christians. There are too many churches in need of action on the part of all the members. Leaders ought not to do things for others what they should do for themselves.

Characteristic Four

The Maieutic Leader is **prepared to give direction and support while allowing ownership by others**.

Don't miss the term ownership as it applies to the

Maieutic leader. It is easy to see with the concept of midwife and coach. Wise leaders in today's dynamic churches will understand the need for ownership.

A healthy church is measured in terms of unity and the number of members who are equipped for ministry. Ownership of activities is a needed step for members functioning in ministry. Today's church can be healthy when the spectator mentality is benched and the members roll up their sleeves and get in the game. No more can we afford the spectator mentality that looks to professionals to perform while the rest sit on the sideline and fume when things don't go as expected.

Ownership means that leaders take seriously the responsibility of equipping God's people for ministry (Ephesians 4:12). They will take a look at all the programs that are currently active and ask tough questions to see if they are accomplishing what they were intended to accomplish. Are they still meeting needs, and are the leaders of these ministries accepting ownership of each part of their work and responding to the labor in appropriate ways? Good leaders initiate programs that help people mature; and then they own the need to change to make them better. "Effective leaders are midwives to ministry because they see to it that Christians are discipled and equipped to fulfill their purpose in the world, according to God's plan" (James Means).

Paul told Timothy that leaders were to "*direct the affairs of the church*" (1 Timothy 5:17). Overseers may take too much administration of a program. Pastors may take too little. Maieutic leaders will know just how much to take, and they will insist on ownership. "*If anyone does not know how to manage his own family, how can he take care of God's church?*" (1 Timothy 3:5).

Characteristic Five

The Maieutic Leader uses communication skills to involve others.

Leaders can talk and listen. When they talk, they will need to have something definite to say. When they listen, they will need to listen with all systems. Sometimes what is not said is more important than what is said.

Using an approach which is known as "The Discovery Bible Study" might make the point more vivid. This approach uses three steps. Step One: Gather the information. Step Two: Analyze the information. Step Three: Apply the information.

In the gathering stage the leader will listen to all involved members and use the Socratic method of asking questions. During this stage the leader is not offering opinions or judgment. He is interested only in the condition of the patient or program. Brainstorming can serve as a valuable tool in this stage. Questions that can be asked: "What is your program?" "What is its purpose?" "Where is it working?" "Where is it not working?" "Who is involved in it?" "What other program does it impact?"

During the Analysis stage leaders will search out what is happening and why. Here we would look at causes and underlying issues. Sitting down and leading a discussion about the specifics of a program and what the involved persons are feeling will help the leader help the involved persons utilize all their gifts in taking a program in a satisfying direction. During this stage the leader will help the group look at the resources at their disposal, personnel needs, and boundaries.

Good Maieutic leaders will allow the group to generate plans for managing the program and the process. There may be a need for pruning at this time. After the group analyzes the task, it is time to move to the next step.

The third step is the plan on paper. Many plans will be discussed, but the plan that the group decides on is the one that gets on paper. If you can't write it on paper, it is not clear. The midwife will work in conjunction with the expectant mother to make the best plan for the big occasion. With the help of the people involved in the program, Maieutic leaders will select the best plan likely to bring out the best possible outcome for the event.

One of the great tragedies of the modern church is communication breakdown. Somewhere between the plans and the carrying out of those plans is a communication gap the size of the Grand Canyon. An old preacher of years gone by used to say that his sermon was simple: "I tell them what I'm going to tell them. I tell them. Then, I tell them what I told them."

A wise leader will develop and use good communication skills to involve others. Sometimes this can be done publicly in the assembly or through a publication, but it is best done person to person. Leaders will need to meet regularly with different ministries in their flock and spend a lot of time listening and leading discussions so that all members will feel that they are being heard.

Characteristic Six

A Maieutic leader **takes responsibility until others can assume it**.

As in the case of the midwife, a wise leader will accept the responsibility at the beginning. He will get things ready and take charge while he assesses the situation. Once the assessment is made, other people can move toward assuming their ownership of the activity.

It is vital at this stage not to take over and run the program. If this happens, leaders will have the program in their laps for some time to come. Burnout will occur and others will have to rework the activity. Analysis of the situation will allow the leader to equip gifted individuals for this work of ministry.

In a situation where there is chaos, the leader might have to take on more responsibility until things settle. The authoritative leader will need to take a lot of control until the time that others can assume it. But don't be fooled into thinking that one leader or a small group of leaders can accomplish as much as a hundred men and women working in harmony. For a birthing event to take place, each person must fulfill his or her responsibility. The quicker leaders can move good, gifted members into a program, the quicker the work of ministry can be carried out.

Characteristic Seven

A Maieutic leader **empowers others**.

A good leader can learn to lead others to think and plan. Part of the "Equipping Ministry" will be found in leaders who can lead by example and never command or manipulate. A Maieutic leader is not one who thinks for others, but one who assists people to think for themselves.

Leaders are to work for people's maturity, not for their dependency.

Good leaders do not strive for power, except the power that empowers others.

What are the things that impede my flock from getting the best nourishment and receiving their daily exercise? How can we enhance the individual development of our sheep while increasing their power? When we create a climate that encourages free exchange of ideas, we will see that participation is cultivated, and we are more likely to see our flock empowered to greater service.

Each of these characteristics is intended to give the reader a picture of what can happen when leaders combine the Bishop/Overseer and the Pastor/Shepherd models. I hope that I have written enough in this chapter to give you a vision of what biblical leadership can be if there is a Maieutic approach to leadership in the local church.

I would want the reader to look again at the leadership style you are now modeling. Is this old/new style of leadership Biblical, and will it help us lead churches to greater service for the Master?

Discussion Questions

1. How would you explain Maieutic leadership to someone who has never heard of it?

2. How would Maieutic leadership affect your congregation?

3. What is one thing that will change in your leadership as a result of reading this book?

Bibliography

Anderson, Dr. Lynn: *They Smell Like Sheep*

Covey, Stephen R.: *The 7 Habits of Highly Effective People*

Doherty, William: *Take Back Your Marriage*

Eichman, Nancy: *Keeping Your Balance*

Fisher, Roger and Ury, David: *Getting To YES*

Gates, Bill: *Business @the Speed of Thought*

Gerig, Donald and Litwiller, Gary: Leadership Magazine, Summer, 1992, P. 76

Hummel, Charles E.: *The Tyranny of the Urgent*

Luecke, David and Southard, Samuel: *Pastoral Administration*

Malony, H. Newton: *When Getting Along Seems Impossible*

Maxwell, John: *The 21 Indispensable Qualities of a Leader*

Ranier, Thom S.: *Surprising Insights From the Unchurched and Proven Ways to Reach Them*

Short, Mark: *Time Management for Ministers*

Williams, Dennis E. and Gangel, Kenneth O.: *Volunteers for Today's Church: How To Recruit and Retain Workers*

Feedback on this text is welcome and encouraged. Please contact James@burnschurchofchrist.org with your comments!

Made in the USA
Charleston, SC
10 September 2016